DEDICATION

This book is dedicated to people using their skills, talents, and abilities to make a positive difference in the world by pursuing their purpose with passion. We hope you are inspired and encouraged to persist through all adversities and obstacles along your path.

TESTIMONIALS

"This book is unarguably the definitive narration of man's experiences on earth. It holistically encompasses topics such as success, love, persistence and faith while teaching trailblazing lessons on life. The authors go a long way towards promoting positivity and purpose as being fundamental for a productive life. This is not just a splendid book; it is a spectacular one and can only be described as a labour of dedication, a fastidiously researched and profusely illustrated account of personal experiences. There are highly inspirational excerpt as each chapter takes took a unique journey. I definitely feel that this book should be shared globally to touch readers and be a source of encouragement."

-Dainelle Mc Lean

"Journeys to Success: Napoleon Hills inspired stories was deeply moving. These stories inspire and can help change your life. The principles applied in the stories have helped these people to achieve their dreams by overcoming obstacles.

The power of belief and to never give up on your dreams as the stories in this book have demonstrated is an essential theme. Focusing on the finish line and believing in yourself will get you to the end of the race and truly be a winner in many facets of life. Thank you Napoleon for inspiring so many and providing us with the tools in your toolbox. "

-Barbara Hollander

Calabasas, CA

Entrepreneur

Director of Silent Auctions for Philanthropy &

Representing Michael Grandinetti Magic, GPA Entertainment, SixTwentySix Productions

"This is a book of insight, love and empowering wisdom. Which allows one to envision the possible and be woken to the infinite human potential.

As your soul embraces the journey of another soul, you are strengthened through their experience."

-Daniel James Bax, Inspirational Speaker, Author and Breakthrough Recovery Coach (Author of The LIFE of Your CHOICE)

"This book reminds me that my vulnerability, or my ability to be vulnerable is a part of my life's success puzzle. It also reminds me that my thoughts create my beliefs, and my beliefs create my reality. Beautifully written, indeed."

-Sheena Blake

Discovering Diversity Publishing

"I'm a life long learner and I read a lot. This collection of personal stories and insights have served me well over the last while because my life and career took a big turn and I needed this. Because personal and professional success is a daily trek into the unknown, books like this are so important. They become the confirming voice in our head that says: "see, you can do this". They are the hand we hold when our stomach quakes after a big decision. They become the pick-me up when we're lying face down after a risky move didn't turn out so good. That's life and that's business. I love reading personal 'aha' stories and these ones are keepers for sure. Enjoy."

-Tina Overbury

http://tinaolife.com/

"What a gift it was to read these stories. This is a brilliant collection of how ordinary people overcame their situations to find a place of peace, fulfillment and understanding. Inspiring, honest and real."

-Alison Donaghey

DominoThinking.com

I had the honor to be a contributing author in Volume 1 of the Journeys to Success series and I am proud to be a part of a franchise that has continued with the same sort of excellent content in Volume 2. You will laugh, you will cry but most importantly you will be inspired to carry on through whatever trials and tribulations life throws at you. It's hard to imagine what some people have to endure in their lives but it's authors like these who show us the way through to the other side!

-Tom Sutter

Partner/VP - Sales & Business Development, Crum-Halsted Insurance

Co-Founder/Board Chair, Cal's Angels – calsangels.org

Author – bitterorbetterbook.com

Resiliency is the ability to overcome adversity. It is something that is innate in all of us and yet we have moments and experiences that has doubted this ability all the time. I am overcome with curiosity and overcome with senses of familiarity as I read these stories. The world is bigger and better than the day to day we live in. These stories are testimonies of lived experience that provide guidance and opportunities for us to reflect on our existence, passions and humanity. Every lesson is learned and earned. In a world where we are often told we are not enough; these stories remind me otherwise. It is only in us and within us that transformation can happen first. Then we can transform the world.

-Chhaya Chhoum,

Executive Director at Mekong NYC

I have been developing and running my own businesses for 25 years. Success requires perseverance, perseverance requires motivation and motivation requires inspiration. This book provides that inspiration. These are the stories of people who never gave up. Their stories are a guiding light to anyone who has struggled on the road to fulfilling their dreams.

-Shannon Adams

Entrepreneur

ACKNOWLEDGMENTS

Dear Reader,

It is an honour to have been asked to formally acknowledge the many contributors that have made this book possible.

I first witnessed Bob Proctor speaking on stage at a low point in my life, while I was seeking some meaning in life and a way forward on my path, possibly like you if you are reading this book. Bob has impacted millions of people by sharing a powerful message of hope, by changing your thoughts you can transform your life.

When Tom asked, Bob did not hesitate in accepting the request to write the foreword and it is an honour for us all to have him take part in this publication.

Thank you Bob Proctor for leading the way in this journey.

Compiling the book was a journey in itself and could not have happened without the guidance of Tom Cunningham. If you have searched for success stories of Napoleon Hill, you can not fail to have come across him. He has been a true guiding light throughout this journey, taken us (the authors) to task, kept us on track and encouraged us with a vision to make this his best book to date.

Tom encompasses the principles of Napoleon Hill. He has made it a mission to not only share his own story but to highlight outstanding individuals around the world through his Journey to Success radio show and now this series of books.

Thank you Tom Cunningham for your vision in manifesting Journeys To Success.

When you read our stories you will notice that what brings us together is that guiding light and a search for inspiration to keep moving forward despite the odds.

Brad Szollose has been selfless in designing a cover image to represent this togetherness, the cover has captured what this book means to all of us, but also serves as a symbol of hope to you and everyone that reads this book.

Thank you Brad Szollose for your creativity in creating the perfect book cover.

Every Journeys To Success author embraced the principles of Napoleon Hill and they transformed their lives. His works have been like a road map sharing exactly what was possible and because of him, we are able to share hope with others.

I would like to thank Napoleon Hill and also acknowledge the Napoleon Hill Foundation, for continuing his good works. You are a true global and generational legacy.

Having written my own chapter, I know how much of a personally emotional journey this has been, I thank God for providing the inspiration that helped me write Perfectly On Purpose. I would like to acknowledge my Co-Authors for sharing your most intimate moments with the world so we can inspire others.

Thank you Tony Rubleski, Bill Hoffman, Fauna Hoedi, Jim Shorkey, Diana Dentinger, Andreas Jones, Nigel Wall, Paul Guyon, Norma Edmond, J. Ibeh Agbanyim, Tony Fevola, Ana Fontes, Craig Kules, Daniel Zykaj, Shaniequa Washington, Shamla Maharaj, Gina Best, Nancy Lee, Amy Thomson and Dionne Malush.

Last but not least, I would like to say a special thanks to our publisher, John Westley Clayton, for taking the leadership, vision, creativity and inspiration of all the contributors and working endlessly to transform it into Journeys to Success Volume 2, a book we are all proud to be a part of.

I hope that this book will serve as your guiding light in difficult times and a reminder that you will make it in the end. If you have not yet made it, it is not the end. In fact, this page and this moment, is only the beginning.

With Love and Wisdom,

Sophia Bailey

www.PerfectlyOnPurpose.com

FOREWORD

By: Bob Proctor

"Do not wait: the time will never be 'just right'. Start where you stand, and work whatever tools you may have at your command and better tools will be found as you go along."

-Napoleon Hill

I'm a big fan of Napoleon Hill. For over 55-years his words have impacted me at a deep and profound level. Not a day goes by where I don't use or share his wisdom in my life and with others throughout the world. As a speaker, author, consultant, coach and mentor in the personal development industry for over 40-years I can tell you that everyone has a story. Some are amazing, some are good, some are average, and far too many read like a tragedy full of lost dreams, lost hope and so much lost potential for good.

The book that you now hold in your hands or read on the screen is a book about decisions and choices. Each of the contributors in this book faced a major decision or crisis at some point or at multiple times within their life. Unlike the overwhelming majority of society that either quits or turn in the keys to their dream at the first sign of setback, they became the minority of individuals that pushed on and achieved success when few, even themselves, often doubted and believed it could even be possible. Their stories are memorable. Their journeys inspirational. Their positive influence on thousands of others is worth studying and applying within your own life.

Let's go back in time to my own personal journey to success as I could easily relate to many of the people who bared their souls in this book. It was

1961 and I was introduced to the classic book Think and Grow Rich by the late Napoleon Hill. Up until this point in time my life journey was lackluster, full of fear, and gripped by the realization that I still had far too much month left after my paychecks were cashed. I was floundering. Searching. Restless. Hanging on by a thread.

Then, on a fateful day in 1961 my friend Ray Stanford changed my life by sharing this book with one simple instruction: read it daily and follow the advice within its pages. I did and soon mustered up the courage and faith to leave a cozy and secure job as a fireman for a life of adventure and financial independence. Leaving the safe harbor was scary but staying put seemed like an even worse way to finish out my remaining days. Yes, like everyone you'll meet and become inspired by in this incredible book, Napoleon Hill's book and teaching was the launch pad that turned my life around and forever changed my destiny for the better!

You'll discover that every single contributor in this book faced intense adversity and short-term setback, but flipped it into powerful lessons to gain strength from other positive role models and from the words penned by Hill's book Think and Grow Rich. While they each have their own path on the road of life, the markers to guide them to more fulfillment are also contained in the success system Hill observed and chronicled from hundreds of other men and women who successfully completed their missions while writing his book.

While Napoleon Hill passed away in 1970, his powerful and timeless words have and still continue to influence hundreds of thousands of people from around the world. Here are three key things to pay particular attention to within the stories you will be reading:

#1: Why a person's mindset must be carefully nourished and protected each day

#2: Why clarity and taking action now, regardless of the present situation, is the vital difference between success and achievement

#3: The power of persistence and learning from each setback and achievement along the way

It is my belief that if you follow the masses, you're really going to be in a mess. Why? Because the masses have no idea where they are going? They've got to wait to turn on the news to see what kind of day it is. They look out the window and say, "Oh my, well this is going to be a bad day for traffic." Why not look at it differently? Each of the people in this book not only looked at their life and situation differently, but they also modeled those already living a successful life they wished to achieve.

So, as you prepare to meet the first person in chapter one and discover their own Journey to Success I remind you that the world's most successful people are all able to make decisions. Decision makers go to the top and those who can't make decisions seem to go nowhere. Think about it. You made a decision to invest in this book. Use it wisely as the nuggets of wisdom in each chapter are anchored in success principles that have stood the test of time. You are fortunate to have found such a book as this and I commend and applaud Tom Cunningham for bringing these stories together in this second book.

I wish you continued abundance and vitality on your own journey to success. Congratulations on investing in the most important thing in the world: your mind.

-Bob Proctor

INTRODUCTION

Napoleon Hill is a global brand and the most recognized name in the personal development industry worldwide. My website attracts visitors from over 130 countries every month from people searching for Napoleon Hill.

Hill's book, Think and Grow Rich, has sold over 100 million copies since it was first published in 1937. It has been translated into many languages and published in many countries. It is one of the Top 10 Bestselling Books of All Time. His other classic book, Law of Success, is also a classic.

This volume of Journeys To Success: Napoleon Hill Inspired Stories is the second in what will become a series of books co-authored by people from all walks of life and many countries. This volume has contributors from 7 countries.

The co-authors of this edition open up their lives to share their story of how they have used Napoleon Hill's 17 Principles of Success in their lives to pursue their purpose and goals.

Both the stores and the authors are diverse however they share one thing in common – a desire to encourage you in the pursuit of your own Purpose and Goals using timeless success principles that have been credited with creating over one million millionaires.

Once again, as with volume 1, Brad Szollose, author of Liquid Leadership, designed the front and back cover and John Westley Clayton, a Napoleon Hill Foundation Certified Instructor is the book's Publisher. They are both committed to making the Journeys To Success book series one that will inspire and encourage people from around the world to discover and pursue their Purpose and Goals using Hill's 17 Principles of Success.

The co-authors would love to hear from you and help you in whatever way they can and have provided their contact information so you can reach out to them.

If you would like to contribute a chapter for one of the upcoming volumes of Journeys To Success, please contact me at tom@tom2tall.com for details.

-Tom "too tall" Cunningham

Founder of the Journeys To Success book series

Napoleon Hill Foundation Certified Instructor

MWR Life Inspiration Ambassador

Founder of Journey To Success Radio

CONTENTS

TRAILBLAZING LESSONS ON THE JOURNEY TO SUCCESS

By: Tony Rubleski

Note: This is from the latest book in the bestselling Mind Capture series titled: Mind Capture: Leadership Lessons from Ten Trailblazers Who Beat the Odds and Influenced Millions, by Tony Rubleski.

trail-blaz-er:

1. One that blazes a trail.

2. An innovative leader in a field; a pioneer.

It started with a phone call a couple of years ago. I was on the phone with master marketer, business coach, and fellow author Jim Palmer discussing life, goals, and in particular my next book in the Mind Capture series. I had one idea originally of where the next book would go and its message, while he had another idea for me to consider after a few minutes into our conversation.

I'd been thinking for many months that my next book would be about dealing with setbacks, and the steps used in the mental battle to attack and overcome them. As many in my inner circle of close friends, family and business associates already knew, I'd seen enough chaos, change, and unforeseen disruption the last few years to make people's jaws drop. I'm not proud of it all, as it was painful, but it was also necessary to break free and grow to a much higher progression point of long-term happiness. This isn't mentioned to ask for sympathy or air all of my dirty laundry, but frankly to set up the context of my thoughts and mindset behind the book.

As many of you know, when life throws intense challenges and adversity your way, it can and will test every ounce of mental, physical, and spiritual muscle you thought you'd ever possessed. It also shows you that you have great reserves of ingenuity and untapped creativity that can be dug up from hidden places within you, that you likely didn't imagine existed until the moment of crisis appeared.

Let me quickly go back to my phone call with Jim. As we wrapped up our intense conversation, my direction for the original book I had planned writing did a complete 180-degree turn. I'd almost forgotten that an incredible gold mine of wisdom and success strategies was sitting on my laptop and saved audio files, which I had accumulated the past seven-years from many of the best sales, marketing, leadership, and newsmakers on the planet.

This gold mine of wisdom contained over 80+ taped phone interviews that I'd compiled for my paid monthly newsletter subscribers. Since I'm always under multiple deadlines, I'd frankly taken for granted the wisdom, tips and inspiration contained in the interviews with my trailblazing and highly enlightened guests.

A quick rewind back in time to late 2010

It was mid-December and I was sitting in the basement of my home. The downstairs living room had become my new bedroom and short-term bachelor pad the last 3-months as I sat in limbo figuring out if I or my soon to be ex-wife would be the first to move out. Her house was upstairs; mine was now the basement. As I sat on the basement couch on this cold December evening signing advance copies of my third book near the stack of waiting envelopes, my mind was focused on the task at hand. Not pretty, no delegating, just an urgency to get the books and media kits out the door before Christmas and New Year's came crashing in.

The pre-launch book marketing of the third Mind Capture book was in full swing. The advance copies and book related promotional items would go to select peers and fellow book reviewers in advance of the official release date of February 2011. Getting the book to clients and fans could no longer be delayed.

Regardless of the fact that my marriage was burning down around me, the mission had to be completed after months of delays due to this major life crisis. I kept thinking in my mind the entire time as I worked from the basement couch, if my peers, clients, and mentors could see the circumstances of my life now and how they'd dramatically changed for the worst during the last 6-months, I'm certain many would be shocked. At the same time many would say, "Oh, we've been in your shoes. Welcome to the club called adversity."

After about 2-hours of signing books, licking envelopes and finishing the last package I got up from the couch to grab a glass of water. When I walked back towards the stack of freshly packaged books, I felt a strong urge to grab my cell phone and take a picture of the 50 envelopes that had just consumed my time. As I held up my phone in my right hand and snapped the digital picture, I smiled, and then a few seconds later began to feel a deep sense of sadness. It was the strangest emotion I'd ever felt: joy quickly followed by incredible sorrow.

I had decided in late September that due to the delay of a pending divorce, I'd bypass the traditional New York publishing route of 12-18 months to produce and release a book. I'd go back to the early days and return to my roots of self-publishing. I was excited to share the message, even though my personal life and ambition were daily crumbling down around me like falling buildings. The stress of the divorce was doing its best to take away my mind, passion, and energy. It's horrifying to feel like your life is stuck in quick sand and after many months of unhappiness I knew something finally had to change.

I mention this story in the beginning of this book and the picture I took from that night in mid-December of 2010, as it would serve as a powerful reminder that no matter what was happening in my life, I would press on and keep moving in spite of feeling that on far too many days throwing in the towel and quitting would be the best thing to do.

Napoleon Hill talks about the importance of persistence in all of his teaching and in great detail in his classic book Think and Grow Rich. This trait is not only vital to possess, but to also employ and use each day on our own personal journey to success and happiness. I found myself during the divorce process having to dig deep into my soul and read his books with a new sense of urgency like I'd never experienced. Yes, I'd read many of Hill's books, but now I was smack dab in the middle of intense fear and doubt.

They Say the Darkest Hour is Just Before Dawn

I've found myself over the last few years systematically questioning everything about the first 43-years of my life. The "American Dream" as I had envisioned it would look during a 14-year marriage was gone. The new house, new cars, horses, stability, and the happy nuclear family for my three children were also gone. Finished, Over, an illusion that ended in divorce. The amount of mixed and painful emotions played havoc on my mind for many months during the fall of 2010 and continued into 2011.

Now that I knew chapter one of life was over, what would chapter two look like? What would I do next? What direction would I take and pursue? Would I live in the past and the land of regret, known as "could've, would've or should've?" Would I choose the common path of staying paralyzed and in neutral for months, years or possibly the rest of my life? Or...would I move into the land of possibility known as chapter two of life? These were tough, yet necessary questions to ask myself. Finding the answers to these questions with a wounded mind and spirit was a daunting challenge indeed.

I was at a crossroads moment in life at age 38 with cloudy vision, a tornado of emotions swirling in my mind, and a lack of immediate answers to this new challenge. With a pending divorce involving four other lives, and a business to try and keep afloat at the same time, I was frankly terrified. The stress, sorrow and doubt were nothing like I'd ever experienced before or had thought was humanly possible.

"Faith is taking the first step, even when you don't see the whole staircase."
-Martin Luther King, Jr.

It was in the fall of 2011 when my divorce was final that my mind began to ignite again like a Phoenix rising from the ashes. They say that time heals old wounds and it is a very true statement if we look ahead and not just in the rear view mirror of life known as the past. I was now spending a lot of time in the Pacific Northwest meeting lots of new and positive people and picking up the pieces from the fallout during the last 18-months.

I have to admit my third book which released 9-months earlier in the beginning of 2011 got lost in the shuffle of great change and frankly due to my own loss of faith in what the future might even look like. Dealing with attorney's, judges, and dividing things up and now only seeing my kids on a limited basis tore me up inside. Fortunately, I went back and reread my own book and discovered that its positive message and my own increasing confidence were the right combination to get back on my feet to once again do what I loved more than anything else: teaching and sharing positive information with other people.

With my confidence surging again, the old Tony combined with the new Tony began to take shape. I thank God for his providence and timing. Yes, a large door had shut, but many new doors of opportunity had also opened up at the same time. As I reflect back now, multiple miracles had visited me when I least expected them to show up or frankly even believed could still exist.

As 2011 came to an end I noted that at many times it felt like my life was a dream. Especially on long flights, the quiet hours at 36,000 feet gave me a much-needed reprieve from the hustle and stress of life below on planet Earth. Yes, my life was coming along better now. I was healing each day but I was still processing the pain of loss and impact that the recent divorce was having on my three children. In addition, it felt like my writing and speaking career was starting all over again. I often found myself asking these two questions,

1. Was all the time away writing and traveling to share my gifts worth it?

2. Did I shortchange those closest to me?

As 2011 was in its final hours, I found myself 2000-miles away from Michigan on New Year's Eve in downtown Spokane, Washington. Stepping outside of a friend's condo onto their deck, I stopped, leaned on the rail and slowly watched the fast rushing river 40-yards below me. As I listened to the water, and looked at the moonlit sky for a few minutes, a profound realization struck my mind: after a long season of darkness and uncertainty in late 2010, a year later I was back in the game again and damn it felt good!

Yes, there were still issues to work on but the huge stack of guilt, doubt, and regret was slowly clearing away in my mind one day at a time. The fog of fear was beginning to dissipate and it was now time to plug back into my goals and dreams to jump back into the game of life.

With a renewed sense of vigor and passion I was once again attacking the bookshelf, questioning, dreaming, thinking big again, and waking up happier each day on a new search to rediscover who I really was and where chapter two of life could go. With my outlook brighter the right ideas began to assemble faster, doors began to swing open again, and the right people began to show up. What my mentors, alive and those who'd passed on, had said time and time again about the power of a positive mental attitude wasn't a pipedream, it was real.

What we focus on we get. Thank God we have a choice in the matter and don't have to allow temporary setback, delays, or short-term failure stop us from getting back up off of the ground and moving forward.

I firmly believe that when life turns chaotic and setback rears its unpredictable head, we have a choice: we can either choose to get better from the experience or we can get bitter and negative by allowing excuses, anger, and resentment to take hold of our mind and spirit. The divorce and list of new challenges had obviously humbled me in many ways, but at the same time it would be the biggest test to see if what I'd read, lived, taught, wrote about, and practiced most of my life still made sense after an extremely difficult two-year period.

Would I quit and walk away from writing and speaking? Settle in and get a job to play it safe? Or, would I regroup, refocus and get back on the offensive? This book is one of my answers to those very questions.

The Good News:

We're Allowed to Reinvent Ourselves Each Day, Forgive Ourselves and Others and Shut the Door to the Past

Many of you reading can relate to what I'm saying. Maybe it's the loss of a loved one, a business, a dream, a cancer diagnosis, a child, a job you loved, or some other sucker punch that completely threw you for a loop. It knocks you down many times in mind, spirit and body and tries to keep you stuck there in the pit of despair. However, as the pain resides, the confidence and momentum can return if we forgive, grow, and change our thinking. When this happens, life and passion can return and we heal forward into a new season of life. One season ends and another one starts anew. We're never quite the same as time, growth, new people, and wisdom have reshaped us into a much different person.

Why Positive Influences are So Important, Especially Today

Let's face it; we ALL need more positive influences and people in our daily lives. I've had many people tell me, "Tony those interviews you do are incredible!" While it would be easy to sit on my press clippings and fanfare, I've arrived at a point in life where that's no longer the primary driver to what I do to serve others. My core mission or "why" is big, bold, direct and massive: help expose millions of people per year to positive, life-changing information.

The media landscape is built on fear and controversy. Complaining is epidemic and toxic. Blame is the new game. Add in a growing push for entitlement at all levels of government and within the media, the "something for nothing" syndrome is putting more people within society on edge. It's not a conspiracy or a paranoid dream. It's happening and people are waking up!

I see it around the world, at my events, on conference calls, as the game of fear is being exposed. People know that deep down something has gone astray. They've ignored their intuition too long, buried their dream, and have allowed the fear peddlers to sell them a vision of life that no longer makes any sense. After years of societal programming and norms that no longer work in a digital-based open world, the addiction to negativity and

8

traditional job/career/retire after 30 years career model has been exposed and dismantled especially by the 20-30 year old crowd. Frankly, most people are sick of the old model and looking for ways to improve their life, those that they love, and others they'd like to serve with greater reach and impact.

Why This Book and its Message at This Moment in Time?

The last several years I've been blessed to pick the minds of many of the top leaders, thinkers and influencers on the planet. I know that the time I share during the interview with my guest and the research involved in the process is valuable for everyone involved.

I still get a charge out of interacting and engaging with my special guests and never take their time and wisdom for granted. Each of them has a unique story and a journey that teaches us lessons from both sides of the wheel of life when it seems everything is clicking, or when it seems all hope of achieving our goal seems too far away or even impossible.

Each person interviewed in the book comes from diverse, eclectic and oftentimes mundane backgrounds. The commonality, however that they ALL share is massive amounts of persistence! What would knock 99 out of 100 people out of the game from even trying to pull off, they simply refuse to accept and continue to press on. With relentless intensity, the pull to achieve is simply too strong, and eventually after years of toil, sweat, heartache, and an emotional roller coaster, many of them "arrive" to the surprise of the casual observer. Even with the chorus of dream-stealers, doubters and sadly, the criticism of those nearest, including families and friends, they persisted onward through thick and thin.

The road to their seemingly overnight success is often times littered with years of failed enterprises, tears, and pain from many outdated relationships that simply couldn't handle the stress brought on by lack of security, stress, a steady pay check, and maxed out credit cards. This is the side of being an entrepreneur that few talk about. In addition, the "crazy idea" that they chased was made even more tempting to leave when taking a steady job with benefits, was often simply a phone call or email away from eager employer's looking for someone with their talent and drive to come work for their organization.

For example, when the accolades come and success finally arrives in the eighth year of being in business, it's amazing how quickly people want to skip over or ignore the first seven years of the story. Those were the lean years, when few, if anyone, that knew what they were really up to, believed in them. The amazing thing is that as they persisted and made adjustments along the journey, they were also being forged from raw iron (their vision) into steel (the successful outcome).

The last several years I've been extremely fortunate and blessed to pick the brains of some of the brightest minds on the planet ranging from the fields of sales, marketing, psychology, to sports, music and spirituality. It hasn't come easy to 'Capture' these incredible minds on the phone. I put in the time, the discipline, the miles, the thousands of pages read, to do my homework and establish a track record with busy PR handlers and agents. The mission is to make them look good while at the same time insuring that my guest feels relieved that they didn't waste their time.

Each guest knows within the first 5-minutes that our interview will be different than most others they often do. I know this to be true as others also interview me as an author myself. At the end of our time together on the phone I want to pull out not only multiple nuggets of wisdom for my audience, but also something so unique that it leaves them thinking as they hang up the phone, Damn, I did not expect that. That was unique, engaging, and memorable.

Here's the secret that shocks most people that ask me about my interview guests: they are regular people just like you and me that have achieved massive success in their respective fields. They all had to start somewhere and often times it was during times of great chaos and setback taking place within their own lives that they made the big decision, to cut the cord and go full throttle after their big goal or dream.

Nothing was given to them. They had to hustle, deal with lots of rejection, and bust through the paradigms of what a long line of others said couldn't be done. They also had to face down, and conquer the twin enemies known as fear and self-doubt often times for years in relative obscurity and during multiple setbacks. During this process, each of them grew, blazed a trail, and changed millions of lives along the way for the better.

While each Trailblazer is unique and talented in their own way I went back through the book several times and realized that they all share a few commonalities worth noting. The checklist below with seven key characteristics they possess isn't a magical shortcut to success, but a blueprint of consistent behaviors and habits one will likely need to possess in the pursuit of their own major goal or dream. The list also serves as a powerful reminder that a positive mindset is of monumental importance.

Seven Key Characteristics ALL of These Trailblazers Have in Common:

#1: Intense curiosity

#2: Persistence

#3: Vision

#4: Life-long learners

#5: Problem solvers

#6: Focus on their strengths

#7: Thick skin

What Else You Will Discover in This Book and Full Audio Interviews

*Leadership lessons to inspire and motivate

*The power of faith along the journey

*Effective ways to deal with business setbacks

*Why a strong mindset is essential to get ahead

*Proven ways to reinvent your business, life, and career

*Why failure is part of the success process

*How to handle adversity and doubt

*Time management tips to get more done

*The twin allies known as persistence and belief

*The power of vision, goal setting, and affirmations

*How to think like a Trailblazer

*How to grow a business in any economy

*Proven ways to turn your ideas into reality

*The power of the mastermind and key strategic business alliances

*Why you must guard your mind from negative people, news, and gossip

A SPECIAL THANK YOU FOR PICKING UP THIS BOOK, JOURNEYS TO SUCCESS:

As a special thank you for purchasing this book I've set aside the opportunity for you to read the first chapter, at NO COST, from my latest book in the Mind Capture series titled: Mind Capture: Leadership Lessons from Ten Trailblazers Who Beat the Odds and Influenced Millions. You'll also get to listen to the first full audio interview with the first Trailblazer featured Seth Godin. Simply visit: MindCaptureBook.com

BIO

Tony is currently the president of Mind Capture Group. His message is designed to help people 'Capture' more minds and profits. He is an in-demand speaker who's given hundreds of presentations the past decade, a strategic business coach, and global event promoter with over 20+ years of experience in the personal development industry.

His second book in the Mind Capture series went #1 in three different business categories with Amazon.com and received stunning reviews from a wide range of leaders in marketing, sales, psychology to academia and multiple New York Times bestselling authors. His latest book in the series is titled, Mind Capture: Leadership Lessons from Ten Trailblazers Who Beat the Odds and Influenced Millions.

His work has been featured in various media outlets ranging from Toastmasters International Magazine, The Detroit Free Press, the FOX TV network, ABC, to CNN Radio, NPR and Entrepreneur Magazine Radio. In addition, he has also served as a Faculty member with both the U.S Chamber of Commerce and CEO Space International.

For More Information, Visit: www.MindCaptureGroup.com

ENTREPRENEURISM IS A LIFESTYLE!
By: Bill Hoffmann

The Entrepreneur bug bit me at an early age. I recall when I was young kid, my parents' insurance agent, Mr. Gary, coming to our house monthly to collect the premium payment. Without automatic debit payments or on-line banking, the practice of going to a customer's house was common back then. However, Gary did not just knock on the door, take the payment, and leave. He would come into our house and actually visited. Gary told stories that fascinated me, he was always smiling, and I really looked forward to him stopping by. I usually ended up talking to him as he walked out to his car. He always seemed to have plenty of time to talk to my parents about any old thing other than insurance, and to me as well. I never felt like a kid annoying an adult. He even treated me to candy or popcorn as we chatted.

When Gary put his briefcase into the trunk of his car, I could not help but to see his golf clubs. One day I asked him why his clubs were in the trunk. He told me that he kept them there because he golfed twice a week. He golfed twice a week…how could that be? I had to ask, "Does your boss know?" His answer is what changed the course of my life. He said he was "self-employed" and did not have a boss. I tried to wrap my head around this concept because it really struck a chord with me. You see my father worked for the same company for 36 years and loved to golf! Yet my father's golf clubs rarely left the back of the garage, never in his trunk. If he was lucky he could sneak out very early once a month on a Sunday morning to go golfing before he met the rest of the family at church. He would never leave work early or go in late to play golf. This was simply not an option. I knew right then I never wanted a

J-O-B, with a B-O-S-S! I was destined to be "self-employed!"

I shared this desire with my dad, and with a chuckle he suggested I cut grass throughout the neighborhood. This was a great idea with one problem. We lived in middle class suburb and most of our neighbors cut their own grass. Additionally, I also had three friends who received the same suggestion from their fathers. Consequently, we were competing with one another for the very few yards remaining. To make things even worse, in order to sway the home owner to you, we all were all offering our services for less and less money. It got to the point that we were almost paying the neighbors to let us mow their grass. This made no sense and this very scenario is how I became an entrepreneur at 12 years old! I decided to get my three friends together and developed a plan. My job was to secure the lawn mowing jobs at a fair rate, collect the money and pay them on a weekly basis. They would cut the lawns (including mine) once a week. Because my time wasn't spent with mowing the lawns, I was able to expand the business. I demonstrated to other neighbors what a great job my three friends were doing and explained how this service would benefit them, thus giving them time to do activities that were more enjoyable. With more customers, my friends and I made more money, but I never had to cut another lawn again. These experiences lead me down the entrepreneurial path and gave me the confidence I would need later in life.

I was not always my own boss. Like most students, throughout high school and college I had part-time jobs. While I was thankful for the work, the desire which started years earlier, to be my own B-O-S-S never went away. In fact, working for others helped me recognize the advantages of working for myself, the time freedom, the ability to make what your worth, and more importantly the feeling of calling your own shots. I wanted to be an Entrepreneur and nothing was going to stop me!

After a great out of state college experience, I returned to my hometown, Toledo, Ohio.

It was perfect timing! Like many other Midwest cities in the early 1980's, Toledo was revitalizing its downtown area and was creating an area called Portside, located on the river. The Mayor at the time was searching for an individual/company to create a single issue magazine to highlight all the new restaurants and shops in Portside and draw folks to the adjacent waterfront area known as Promenade Park. The city planned to host weekly concerts and entertainment called "Party in the Park" and wanted the downtown business people and surrounding communities to come down to Portside and Promenade Park for entertainment on Friday nights. I had pulled together a small budget and Toledo Alive Magazine was born in May 1983. The response to this uplifting, fun and insightful magazine was overwhelming, so my one-time publication for the kickoff; Toledo Alive became a monthly magazine available at local outlets and through subscription. Business owners, banks, restaurants and hundreds of retail shops were eager to advertise in this four-color magazine that highlighted the rebirth of Toledo. We had a hit, and I had my own business!

After operating this magazine successfully for four years, I encountered a major obstacle, one that would alter my path for some time. In November of 1987, I began running out of energy and losing weight. I am not talking about mild fatigue; I am talking about having absolutely no energy and losing lots of weight, from 205 down to 163 pounds in less than a month! Being young I felt invincible, I hesitated a bit before making an appointment with my doctor. My doctor quickly observed that I was severely dehydrated and ordered blood work to check my blood sugar level; it was 949, while a normal level is 80 to 120. All he said was, "Put your shirt on, I'm taking you to the hospital." I was diagnosed with Type I Diabetes.

While it was good to know what the issue was, the fact that I had been diagnosed a diabetic was tough! Why me? How could this be? I was very health conscious, worked out all the time, and paid attention to my diet. I was lost in the "it's not fair" mindset. Managing the physical requirements of diabetes was an adjustment, counting carbohydrates, taking five to six shots of insulin a day and of course checking my blood sugar several times a day was a chore. As it turned out, this was the easy part. The mental depression side effects were like a cloud hanging over me, I was a real mess. I stopped working out, socializing, playing tennis, a sport that I loved in college, and I stopped doing what was necessary to operate the magazine. My focus had shifted to self-pity, which turned into self-doubt. My business was suffering and within six months the magazine was on its last leg, I really did not comprehend what was happening; I was too busy feeling sorry for myself. The business was sold and instead of asking myself 'now what?' I found myself saying 'so what?'

My friends and family thought I would snap out of it and my doctor told me that it was normal to feel depressed. This new normal turned into years of just getting by, I had no real purpose. I was working as a limousine driver to pay the bills. I cannot say that being a limo driver was all bad. At times it was great fun and some of the customers were memorable beyond the cute girls, but this truly was just a J-O-B! Speaking of memorable customers, there was a nationally known motivational speaker coming to town by the name of Zig Ziglar. He was to be speaking at the University of Toledo's basketball arena, and since the campus was near my house, I was the driver assigned to pick him up. I owned one of his books, 5 Steps to Successful Selling, yet I cannot say I was excited about the thought of being his driver. The Toledo Express Airport is very small with only one escalator and I remember Zig coming down it, full of energy with a big smile. I reciprocated, just part of the job. He said, "I'm Zig, you must be Bill." I thought to myself, "Must be the name tag."

When I tried to grab his bag, he shared with me that he kept young and spry by carrying his own luggage. "Good for you," I thought. I opened the trunk and he placed his suite case in and asked me if he could sit upfront.

I thought to myself, "You can sit on the hood" I really did not care. Remember, I was in a dark place. As we drove towards Airport Highway, he reached over and turned off the radio. I had to be in this vehicle for 8 hours a day, what was he doing? We continued a few miles down the road in silence and drove pass a cemetery. He then asked me if I could hear it? Then he asked me if I could see it? Honestly, I did not know where he was going with this, yet he was the customer so I kept smiling. He then began telling me that some of the most beautiful architectural buildings, and the most incredible musicals and plays, and the most awesome cures to the worst diseases died with the people in that cemetery. I knew I looked puzzled, he went on to say most people spend their entire lives getting ready, getting set and they never go!

His words hit me like bricks. What was I doing driving a limousine? What should I do next? What happened to my entrepreneurial spirit? When he asked what was holding me back, I knew the answer. I was holding back from life! Another moment with Zig Ziglar affected me as well. Ziglar was not afraid to let his faith be known! He once prayed for a friend of mine that was going through a tough time and he did not seem to care that thousands of people were waiting for him to speak; he told me later that that was more important than getting on stage and speaking, probably why God had him come to Toledo! From that point, I have never been afraid to pray or talk about my faith!

Within two years of meeting Ziglar at the Toledo Express Airport, I was making more money in a month than I had made the entire year that I met him. The difference was I took action, no longer was I getting ready and set, I would just GO!!! One would think that when the money is flowing, all is well. However, something was unsettling in my life. Most people that knew me thought I was very successful, and I was financially. But I was chasing the money, and just like water that seeks its own level, I became comfortable and complacent, I was starting to drift and lose focus. I felt I had no real direction or that I was doing much in the area of growing as a person.

This was a critical revelation. It was not just about the money, I did not feel I was doing what I was born to do. They say hindsight is 20/20, and as I look back, I needed not just to be excited or motivated, I needed a "Definiteness of Purpose."

Nevertheless, as we know, life keeps on moving…I got married, had a child, and another, and another! My family life was hectic and great and I worked hard to be successful and was moving rapidly up the financial ladder. However, there was something deeper I was longing for; I just could not put my finger on it. Perhaps it is because I believe that God is directing my steps that I did not lose faith that I would find my calling. It was in 1999 during a move, that I found a book buried in a box with many other seemingly invaluable items. A book I had never read, let alone even opened. It was "Think and Grow Rich by" Napoleon Hill. I felt called to not only take it out of the box, but to actually begin reading it. After which I could not put it down! I am not sure if you have ever experienced finding a book that made you feel it had been written just for you, but this book spoke to me and I read it several times over the next month. I knew deep down it would set the course I was called to follow. I even started a journal as suggested in the book and I still have it today. This book allowed me to chart a course that no longer focused on my success, my business, my earnings, my happiness, my needs, or me. Instead, my focus was now on how I could help others reach their goals and their dreams. I had always been in the people business, but now I focused on their needs and not my own. My "Definiteness of Purpose" was crystal clear! For the first time in my life, I actually wrote down my goals, and my ultimate goal was to help as many people as possible. To learn and understand that there is a road map, of seventeen universal principals of success and achievement was an "AHA" moment. I had found my mission. Knowing your "Definiteness of Purpose" keeps you on your course, no matter what difficulties arise or what obstacles are in your way. I liken it to the North Star; it always keeps you on track!

From that point on, I'd decided to focus on teaching and sharing this newfound information. I have more energy, more discipline and a bigger why. This laser light focus allows me to accomplish anything that I put my mind to. This erased any thoughts of why I became diabetic or any feelings of not being worthy or not believing in myself. When you have a "Definitiveness of Purpose", it gives you a reason that is bigger than your personal needs or personal desires. I hope and pray that my story can give you the belief that you too can accomplish any dream or goal you have. Just remember it is all about Your WHY!

BIO

Bill is a husband and father of three children. As a matter of fact, his eldest son is currently following in his footsteps!

As a young boy in the Midwest, Bill was raised with the traditional values of hard work, integrity, respect and a great desire to help people. The middle child of five, Bill always had to fight to get his way. That resulted in his incredible competitive spirit that drove him in everything he did. "It's not that I was the best student by nature, but I knew that I wanted to be more than just a young average kid from Toledo, Ohio. I found that sports were a great outlet for me, especially tennis."

Thanks to his tennis, Bill was awarded a full sports scholarship to San Jose State. Following college, he had a short stint as a professional tennis player, before being introduced to network marketing while still in his early twenties. The rest, as they say, is history. Bill went on to build three significant Network Marketing businesses - two as a field leader and one as a company owner.

Along the way, he had built organizations to over 185,000 active team members and customer bases in the hundreds of thousands. After nearly 30 years in the industry, Bill has established himself as a legend of the industry, becoming one of its all-time highest income earners. "With my unique perspective of achieving success both as a rep and an owner, I know that the timing of an opportunity is your greatest asset.

You can reach Bill at billhoffmann@gmail.com or his direct line at 419-466-6399 and www.whynot.gamelootnetwork.com

THE COLOR OF LOVE
By: Fauna Hodel with Jan Hewitt

When I was eight years old, my momma Pretty Jimmie took me to see the movie "Imitation of Life". On that day, I knew I had my own story to tell.

I was raised in Reno, Nevada, by a Black couple who had adopted me, after being approached by a white woman in the ladies lounge of the Riverside Casino. They were told I was of mixed race, with a Caucasian mother and a Black father.

And so I was raised in a Black family, believing I was of mixed race. I was shunned by Blacks for being White, and by Caucasians because I was white-skinned and living with Blacks. I was teased and threatened by schoolmates. I struggled with these issues of racism throughout my childhood, and although Jimmie always did the best she could, the challenge of living in poverty with an adoptive mother who was an alcoholic was on going throughout my childhood and adolescence.

Although Momma and I lived a life full of difficulty, fear and strife, I knew very early on that I wanted to share my story, which advocates kindness. I wanted to broadcast my message that the power of love, kindness and faith will win over hatred, cruelty and anger. And I knew that one day I would make a movie about my story.

Despite the difficulties Momma and I faced each day, I had many people in my life who were such a blessing to me, and who helped me learn to persevere and keep faith. And they taught me so many important lessons.

Jimmie Lee's common law husband Homer Faison was a positive presence for me. He came into my life when I was five, and from him I learned kindness, in a world where kindnesses were few and far between.

My Aunt Rosie introduced me to Napoleon Hill's Success Principles; including "Think and Grow Rich", "Positive Mental Attitude", and "Applied Faith". When I was in my 20's I studied with Joe Green, a philosopher and New Thought Movement preacher. I was working in sales at an art gallery, and working with Joe, using the Napoleon Hill Success Principles, I went from earning $200 per month to up to $7,000 per month. My skills had certainly not improved enough to account for such a huge increase – the change was solely because of studying and putting into practice what I was learning about Napoleon Hill's principles and theories.

Aunt Rosie also introduced me to Reverend Ike, and we would often sit by the radio and listen to his sermons. Reverend Ike was one of the first prosperity gospel preachers, with his theologies "Prosperity Now", "Positive self-image psychology", and "Thinkonomics". Following Reverend Ike was a continuation of my study and realization of the power of positive thinking.

Aunt Rosie was a strong believer in the power of the spoken word – that you can bring something to reality by speaking it and believing in it. I learned this from her and believe it and have practiced it my entire life.

Big Mama, my foster grandmother, introduced me to God and Angels, and gave me strength and courage when I needed it most, and my absolute faith in God and God's Angels has sustained me through all the ups and downs of my life.

Additionally, I went on to study and follow the teachings of Louise Hay about the power of affirmation, and found great strength and courage from her.

These were the people who raised, loved and nurtured me, who taught me about faith and strength, love and kindness.

Upon reaching adulthood, I knew I had to learn about where I came from. I located Tamar, my birth mother, and learned about my biological family and their intriguing and disturbing history.

I was told conflicting stories from different family members, and felt like Erin Brockovich, having stumbled onto a deep and multi-faceted mystery. Some of these stories are contained in my autobiography "One Day She'll Darken".

What I learned was that I am the granddaughter of Dr. George Hodel, who was described by Sheila Weller in Vanity Fair as "the most pathologically decadent man in L.A."

George Hodel was an influential and wealthy surgeon, and his power and reach appear to have had no boundaries. The Hodels lived in the "Snowden House", at 5121 Franklin Avenue in Los Angeles. The house, which is on the L.A. historic register, has a long and unsavory past. In his book "Black Dahlia Avenger", George's son Steve Hodel called the Franklin House a "haunted house of horror", and a mysterious woman who showed up at the house decades later stated, "This is a house of evil".

I was born in 1951 to Tamar Hodel, the Caucasian daughter of Dr. Hodel. Tamar accused her father of incest in 1949, and an arrest and trial followed. After George Hodel was acquitted of incest in a trial that was extremely suspicious (as outlined in Steve Hodel's book), Tamar became pregnant and was sent to St. Elizabeth's Infant Hospital for Unwed Mothers in San Francisco, and I was given away at birth.

Tamar was only sixteen years old when I was born, and in her eyes, Blacks were far more loving than most of the people she encountered in the white community. She wished to ensure that a Black family would raise me, and to that end, she claimed that her new baby's father was Black, and my birth certificate listed the father as "Negro". Her plan worked -- through George Hodel's manipulations and machinations, I was given away under mysterious circumstances to Jimmie Lee and her husband Chris, a Black maid and Black shoeshine man at the Riverside Casino in Reno, Nevada. An official adoption never took place, and the hospital had a 'note' on file saying I was to be given to Jimmie Lee and Chris.

Jimmie and Chris were told that I was of mixed race, (as shown on my birth certificate), with a Caucasian mother and a Black father. I was white-skinned as a newborn, and although they were told I would darken, as I grew older, I never did.

Despite all of the drama and intrigue I stumbled upon when I discovered my biological family, my dream of making a movie about my story remained. And twenty-seven years ago, Napoleon Hill's principles and philosophy drew a person into my life who became my partner to help me achieve my dreams. I recently told her that she is the wind beneath my wings, and the lesson here is that we need this "wind", this collaboration, to make our dreams come true.

Together we worked on the story of my life. I found financing in Hawaii, and we went to Los Angeles and hired a producer.

My dream of sharing my life story was being realized. The project, titled "Pretty Hattie's Baby", was in the early stages of pre-production in L.A., and everything was going well. Our cast was made up of many fine and acclaimed actors, including   Alfre Woodard, winner of numerous Emmy, Screen Actors Guild, and Golden Globe awards, Charles S. Dutton, Alison Elliott, Bobby Hosea, Jill Clayburgh, and Tess Harper.

Then word came that we would have to change the names in the story in order to pass Errors and Omissions. But that was just the beginning – at that time, none of us could have imagined the powerful reach and negative influence of Dr. George Hodel. That is a story in and of itself.

So the names were changed to protect the guilty, and production commenced in Reno, Nevada, Sacramento, California, and Acapulco, Mexico. All involved were amazed at what we were creating.

n Alfre Woodard cited her portrayal of Hattie as her best work

n Director Ivan Passer said of the filming, "There's a miracle every 15 seconds"

n Director of Cinematography Tony Imi: "What happened was pure magic. I tried to make it look as real as possible. It is an exceptional movie, amazing performances. Something magical happened in the entire experience."

n Carmi Gallo, Production Designer: "Pretty Hattie's Baby is a timeless piece"

n Bobby Hosea, actor: "…this is a powerful, beautifully told story of unconditional love, hope, struggle and triumph"

n John Foss of Storyboard Productions: "It's one of the most powerful films I've ever seen".

Principal photography was all but completed, but with just two days of filming to go, the project that was a labor of love came to a grinding halt. And it is almost certain that Dr. George Hodel used his connections and power to have the movie stopped, in order to protect his name. My dream was dashed and I was devastated.

After "Pretty Hattie's Baby" was stopped, I was deeply saddened. Something I had dreamed about my whole life had suddenly and unexpectedly been yanked away from me, when it was so close to being completed and ready for the world to see.

This was the only point in my life where I found it very difficult to continue to think positively. But once I recovered my Positive Mental Attitude, I returned to living moment by moment in faith. And I knew that if I could manifest the movie once, I would do it again. And I was absolutely certain it would happen again.

Through all of this, I was raising my daughters Yvette and Rasha. I had married young, had my first daughter Yvette at the age of 16, and Rasha 11 years later, and my daughters and I grew extremely close because of the many challenges we faced. I poured my love and wisdom into my girls, and my positive outlook on life influenced both of them. Their love and support sustained me through all of our tough times, and will sustain me as I face new challenges. My daughters are smart, kind and compassionate women, and I am extremely proud of both of them – they are my real accomplishments in life.

In the meantime, I carried on with bringing my story to people. In 2008 I wrote and published "One Day She'll Darken", the story of the first 25 years of my life. After the heartbreak and disappointment of "Pretty Hattie's Baby" going off the rails so close to completion, this was a wonderful accomplishment – it was not a movie, but it shared the message I wanted to convey – that love, faith and kindness are stronger than hatred, cruelty and anger.

After my book was published, I worked for Celebrity Society Magazine in Beverly Hills. Celebrity Society is a magazine dedicated to philanthropy and people who pay it forward. While working for the magazine I learned a great deal about the non-profit world, interviewed the heads of many non-profit organizations, and attended countless galas, such as Operation Smile and The John Wayne Cancer Society.

I went on to executive produce my own radio show titled "Fauna's Charity Sizzle Report" on The Amazing Women of Power Talk Radio, and co-hosted "Dare to Dream" with Dr. Anne Marie Evers, the doctor of affirmations.

In August 2015, the Curfman Gallery at Colorado State University hosted "Beyond Color: A Life Journey Using Art to Transcend Culture – The Fauna Hodel Experience", a multimedia exhibit about my experiences with straddling and overcoming racial lines and boundaries. The exhibit explored the numerous artistic links in my life: cinema, fashion, music, writing, architecture, sculpture and photography. This from Donnyale Ambrosine, founder of Culturs.guru, who created and sponsored the exhibit, "We've worked to develop a multi-media journey through the maze of a life with unimaginable twists and turns, and unbelievable characters, with the outcome of delivering a message of love and understanding that transcends race, socioeconomic status, sexual orientation, time and geography."

I currently have a series deal in development with Patty Jenkins, the acclaimed director of the Academy Award winning film "Monster", and the Fantasy/Action film "Wonder Woman", which will be released in 2017. In this series we will tell the story of my life in episodic fashion.

And as of this writing, I am helping to produce a celebrity Tennis Tournament to benefit the Beverly Hills Police Foundation.

I have recently been diagnosed with Stage 3 breast cancer, and am facing this new challenge head on, with the help of my girls. It is frightening and daunting to face the decisions about how to proceed with treatment, but I have firm belief that with the power of love, faith, affirmation, positive thinking, and my many Angels, that I will overcome this new obstacle and win the battle.

I am very grateful to have the teachings of Napoleon Hill, Reverend Ike, and Louise Hay to sustain me. I was blessed by the love and support of those who helped me through my difficult childhood, and I am blessed with the love and support of the people who love me now – all of them have enriched my life beyond what I can describe. So with these principles firmly in place, I face the future with faith, hope and love. And look forward to the next chapter, the next project, the next adventure.

And so I leave you with this message: The human spirit has great ability to overcome adversity, and prevail in the face of difficulty and heartache. At the end of the day, nothing is more important than love, kindness and compassion, positive thinking and affirmation, belief and faith and embracing one another, regardless of differences in race, creed, gender, or sexual preference.

Photo credit: **Elle Zober**

BIO

Fauna was born in San Francisco in 1951 to the Caucasian daughter of Dr. George Hodel, a prominent and wealthy California doctor who was implicated in the Black Dahlia Murder. Fauna was given up at birth under mysterious circumstances to a Black maid and Black shoeshine man at the Riverside Casino in Reno, Nevada.

Raised in the African-American community, she was shunned by Blacks for being White, and shunned by Caucasians because she was white-skinned and living with Blacks. She struggled with these issues throughout her childhood and adolescence, and upon reaching adulthood, located her birth mother, and learned about her family and their intriguing and disturbing history.

Fauna is the Executive Producer and Creative Consultant for the motion picture, "Pretty Hattie's Baby", based on her life story, and the author of "One Day She'll Darken", her autobiography about the first 25 years of her life.

Fauna can be contacted via email at faunahodel@gmail.com

Email: www.FaunaHodelSpeaks.com

Jan Hewitt and Fauna Hodel met in 1990, when Ms. Hewitt worked as Producer Sean Ferrer's assistant on the film "Pretty Hattie's Baby".

Their friendship developed during production of the film, and they kept in touch throughout the years, with Jan helping write copy for several of Fauna's projects. Jan has worked in the automotive industry, the film industry, and the Thoroughbred breeding industry throughout her career, and lives in Lexington, Kentucky.

"BANKRUPTCY IMMINENT"
By: Jim Shorkey

I have read Napoleon Hill's classic book *Think and Grow Rich* 103 times during the past 20+ years. I have read this book like a scientist, cover to cover each time. The version I have read is The Complete Classic Text (published by the Penguin Group; Google The Complete Classic Text). Why would I read the same book 103 times? Why am I going to read it another 103 times during the next 20+ years? Why have I read it 11 times in the past eight months? This does not make sense, does it? Napoleon Hill instructs us on page 119: "Above all, do not stop, nor hesitate in your study of these principles until you have read the book at least three times, for then you will not want to stop." I took this quote as a direct order to me from Napoleon Hill and followed it. I did exactly what he told me to do — exactly! I created incredible success in my life because I followed Napoleon Hill's instructions. After all, he discovered a formula for success. Therefore, when you follow Napoleon Hill's formula, you will succeed in whatever you desire to succeed at. Health? Wealth? Love? Happiness? Spirituality? You choose! I continue to read *Think and Grow Rich* and implement the principles in all areas of my life — and Napoleon Hill's philosophy continues to work every single time. This is my story.

My father died very suddenly of a massive heart attack on March 24, 1996. He literally dropped dead. My mother found him. This was the biggest family tragedy I had ever faced. The pain was overwhelming and yet there was a business to run. In addition to his family, my dad was leaving behind the car business he had been building since 1974. Having been involved in the business for more than 17 years, I thought I was ready to assume command. At the time, I was the General Sales Manager and owned a minority interest in the company. I was prepared — or so I believed. Reflecting back on this time, if I knew half as much as I thought I knew, I would have been pretty darn smart.

In retrospect, I had no clue. I was arrogant. My ego positively got in the way. It was bad enough that I clearly did not know what I was doing. However, what was way worse was that I was convinced I did know what I was doing. I proceeded to operate my dad's business my own way. This was my big chance. I did not want help. I did not want advice. I wanted to make the business bigger than it had ever been. So, here's what happened: Disaster! My business strategies were terrible, each one of them, including marketing, sales, accounting, customer service, leadership and ownership. Really bad! What I quickly discovered was bad strategies always lead to bad results — and my bad strategies led to calamity! (Remember: I really did not know how to successfully run my dad's business.)

In 1998, two years after my dad died, the CPA classification of our family business was bankruptcy imminent. It was 100% my fault and it was an awful feeling. It was bad enough that I had lost my father; now, I was also losing his business. Can you imagine how that felt? I was embarrassed. I felt really bad. I vividly recall that phone call from my sister, Gretchen. She informed me that the bank account was in arrears to the tune of $55,000. Checks were going to bounce, and it was by no fault of hers. This was my responsibility. Needless to say, I did not sleep that night. I was on my bank's doorstep before they opened on Monday morning. I had to face this situation head on, no hiding from the problem. I was so relieved when my banker assured me he would handle the checks. He had been a great friend to my dad, a quality that would continue to benefit me along my journey. I would soon find that my dad had many great friends and that those friends were more than willing to help me. They actually wanted to help. All I needed to do was to be willing to listen. This required humility, believe me. I was moving away from arrogance. I was becoming very, very, very humble. I borrowed $100,000 from my bank to keep the family business floating and then, I got to work. And there was so much work to do.

In 1974, my father started the family automobile business, Courtesy Oldsmobile Jeep. For 22 years, he worked his butt off to survive (initially) and to prosper (in time). The business was my dad's baby, his pride and joy, his dream come true. There was so much blood, sweat, and tears, and also so many great times. My dad created a great business and we always worked hard. My mom, Caroline, worked super hard in the business — always did. (Thank you, mom!) My sister Gretchen, my brother Russell and my brother-in-law Dave Shannon also all worked super hard in our business — they always did. (Thank you Gretchen, Russell and Dave!) In addition to myself, four family members and 40 employees depended on our business to live, eat, vacation and so forth. And now, two years after my father died, the family business was on its way to bankruptcy. Can you imagine that? I was losing. I felt like a loser. It was crushing.

I began reading *Think and Grow Rich* some time from 1995 to 1996. I am not exactly sure when, but I know I was reading it in late 1996 because I remember reading it while waiting in the long lines at Disney World (making my downtime primetime). But even before discovering *Think and Grow Rich*, I began my self-development journey on Sunday, March 1, 1993. I was in a negative state of mind as a result of a disagreement with my brother, Russell. I was decidedly against the idea of self-help. I did not need it. I did not believe in it. I did not want it. I thought it was total crap. But at this time, I had received a promotional cassette tape from Brian Tracy titled, "The Psychology of Selling." I have no idea why I hung onto it. I have no idea why I proceeded to put it into the cassette tape player. I just know that I listened — I really listened! I was blown away. My life changed in an instant and has never been the same since.

I went on to read more than 2,000 books on personal development. I watched videos; I listened to hundreds of cassette tape programs, many from Nightingale-Conant. I did affirmations. I changed whom I was hanging out with. I was obsessed. On December 26, 1993, I stopped drinking alcohol as a result of my studies. (I never drank one drop of alcohol again. Thank you so much, Brian Tracy!) It was during this time that I found everyone was talking about this one particular book — *Think and Grow Rich*. Everyone encouraged me to read it, telling me it was a must read for the serious self-development student. Naturally, *Think and Grow Rich* eventually found its way into my hands. I was quickly discovering that I had so much to learn, so much to internalize. It was a long process.

Now, here is the tricky part: I already had been on a personal development journey for five years when I was told my family business was bankruptcy imminent, a negative $55,000 in the bank account. How could this happen? What went wrong? I was so desperate. I had no place to turn. My back was against the wall. I was going down. I was feeling defeated.

But I did take one crucial step: I decided to commit myself 100% to implementing Napoleon Hill's strategy, without any deviations. You see, up until that moment I had done a lot of reading, but no implementation. I got myself into intense action. On page 14, Napoleon Hill writes: "This book was written for those who seek the rules which have made others successful, and are willing to stake everything on those rules." This is exactly what I decided to do. Was I skeptical? You bet I was! I felt that the book promised way too much. However, I was bankruptcy imminent. What did I have to lose? My feeling was that I had no other choice (and I didn't). On page 13, Napoleon Hill writes: "When riches begin to come, they come so quickly, in such great abundance, that one wonders where they have been hiding during all those lean years." Are you kidding me? I could not even imagine such a thing. However, I pressed on. I was relentless. On page 53, Napoleon Hill writes: "Repetition of affirmation of orders to your subconscious mind is the only known method of voluntary development of the emotion of faith." I did this! I needed to develop faith. I did not have faith.

In 1998, my business barely had a pulse. This is when I began reading *Think and Grow Rich* with intention. I followed Napoleon Hill's instructions down to the smallest details. Remember the quote from page 119? "At least three times." This is what I did. I kept reading. I internalized lessons like those on page 89-90: "Read the entire chapter aloud once every night, until

35

you become thoroughly convinced that the principle of auto-suggestion is sound, that it will accomplish for you all that has been claimed for it. As you read, underscore with a pencil every sentence, which impresses you favorably. Follow the foregoing instruction to the letter and it will open the way for a complete understanding and mastery of the principles of success." I did this! I implemented the "six definite, practical steps" on pages 26-27. I continued doing affirmations. I implemented autosuggestion: "The keystone to the arch of this philosophy (page 89)." I did all of this with so much emotion, exactly as Napoleon Hill directed. You see, I believed Napoleon Hill was speaking directly to me. He was now my mentor. My success needle started to move just a little bit. This gave me hope. I was moving away from skepticism, which was key to discovering success.

I now began to push even harder. I intensified my efforts and the results continued to improve. Without a doubt, the most important lesson I learned from Napoleon Hill was this one: "Seek expert council (page 7)." On page 136, he writes: "First. You are engaged in an undertaking of major importance to you. To be sure of success, you must have plans, which are faultless. Second. You must have the advantage of experience, education, native ability, and imagination of other minds. This is in harmony with the methods followed by every person who has accumulated a great fortune." Napoleon Hill then goes on to say: "Right here is the point at which the majority of men meet with failure, because of their lack of persistence in creating new plans to take the place of those which fail. The most intelligent man living cannot succeed in accumulating money —or in any other undertaking — without plans that are practical and workable. You see, from 1996 to 1998, I had a bad plan. Again, I felt like Napoleon Hill was speaking to me. It seemed like he knew what I had done and he was showing me the way out. So, I started to "seek expert counsel." Wow, did I ever!

I sat down with Malcolm Hamilton, a very successful local automobile dealer. Mr. Hamilton — known as "Mr. Ham" — had been my dad's partner years prior to the development of their individual businesses, and a close friend. He also became a true mentor to me (expert counsel). I asked Mr. Hamilton for a top ten list of the most important things I needed to be doing to become a successful automobile dealer. He gave me a great list.

I also sat down with GMAC, the financial arm of General Motors at the time. They gave me a comprehensive VHS training program (including workbooks) on how to run a successful automobile dealership. Next, I sat down with Chrysler Financial, the financial arm of Chrysler Corporation at that time. They brought in an audit team to analyze my financial statements. They created a targeted action plan to direct me on what I needed to do to turn things around. This was a step-by-step plan of what I needed to fix and how I needed to go about accomplishing each item on the list. One year later, they actually visited again to do the same process and give me a progress report.

Lastly, I sat down with Irwin Bank and Trust. They also gave me great advice. Each one of these people really wanted to help me. Why? Because my father was so well thought of in our industry. My dad developed many great friends over the years and each one of them helped me get out of this mess. (Thank you so much!) Now here is the best part: No charge! All of this help was free! Can you imagine that?! "Seek expert counsel."

I pushed on. I kept reading *Think and Grow Rich*. I kept implementing the instructions I received from Napoleon Hill and believing he was personally mentoring me — and his mentorship grew stronger by the day!

I consulted with the National Automobile Dealers Association (NADA) and I attended a seminar in Boston on how to run an automobile dealership by the "numbers." The instructor was a CPA. What an eye-opener that was! "Seek expert counsel." I joined an automobile dealer industry think tank (these are called Dealer 20 Groups). I read several strategic sales books. "Seek expert counsel." I continue to follow this specific strategy in every aspect of my life today — health, wealth, happiness, love, spirituality. You choose what you want to work on. And here's the knowing that I now have: It works! There is no doubt in my mind.

Napoleon Hill writes, "You must have plans which are faultless." When I began implementing all of these ideas, my success needle began moving in a dramatic way. I was starting to believe in Napoleon Hill. As my belief grew stronger, my success needle moved even more. This led me to faith. As my faith grew strong, my success needle started to really bounce! I kept reading *Think and Grow Rich*. I continued doing autosuggestion every single day and reading my personal statement twice per day (step six, page 26). I kept seeking "expert counsel." I was really intensive on affirmations (and I still am). I was now making a profit. My bank account was growing. I pressed on. I kept reading. Napoleon Hill quotes on page 39: "Desire backed by faith knows no such word as impossible." I have repeated this quote at least 10,000 times! My results kept improving and improving. I was on my way! By the time 1999 ended, my business had accomplished an all-time record profit year. I continued reading and implementing *Think and Grow Rich*.

Initially, I read *Think and Grow Rich* out of desperation. I did not want to go bankrupt. Then, I began reading out of fear. I had moved away from "bankruptcy imminent" and I was so afraid of going back to that scenario. I felt so bad about myself back then. I knew there was no way I was ever going back to that. So, I kept on reading. What would you have done?

Think and Grow Rich is a success formula. On page XIV of the author's preface, Napoleon Hill writes about Andrew Carnegie and his personal implementation of the principles: "By coaching them in the use of this formula, [he] developed in them rare leadership. Moreover, his coaching made fortunes for every one of them who followed his instructions." All I was doing was following Napoleon Hill's instructions. So, I just kept on reading and implementing.

As I write this, it is March 15, 2016. I just finished reading *Think and Grow Rich* for the 103rd time. I have read it 11 times in the last eight months. Today, I read this book with strong faith. You see, I have rewired my brain with self-mastery, self-discipline, and self-control. I know it works. I will continue reading and implementing. This is a book about health, wealth, happiness, love, spirituality — you choose! What do you really, really, really want? You can have it all. Now, please listen, you must do exactly what Napoleon Hill instructs you to do. Let Napoleon Hill be your personal mentor. Read the book from this perspective. You will be amazed! Trust me. This is what I continue to do every single day (ask my wife, Amy) and it works! If it works for me, it will work for you. I just know it will.

These are my results:

1998 = 1 dealership, 40 employees, 800 new and used vehicles sold per year, bankruptcy imminent.

2015 = 6 dealerships, 400 employees, 8,000 new and used vehicles sold per year, prosperity.

I am healthy, wealthy, and happy and I have so much love in my life (most important). I am living my dreams. And all of it I attribute to the instructions I received from my personal mentor, Napoleon Hill. You can do the same. When you do exactly what Napoleon Hill instructs you to do, you will achieve any goal that you are serious about achieving. Believe me!

In conclusion, (1) I am not the smartest guy in the room and I do not need to be. (2) I am an excellent idea thief. I do not believe in re-inventing the wheel. I copy successful people. It's as easy as: "Seek expert counsel." (3) If I can do this, you can do this. I know you can. "Desire backed by faith knows no such word as impossible." Will you make the start?

EPILOGUE

It is March 24, 2016 and I am sitting at our kitchen table, drinking green tea and thinking my thoughts. My sister-in-law (Amy's sister), Zoe Hewitt, has joined me at the table and we have begun a conversation about my self-development journey and, in particular, Napoleon Hill. The discussion has moved to "seek expert counsel" and what that really means. I tell Zoe that I have always felt like Napoleon Hill is speaking directly to me. I often say, "I am not the smartest guy in the room" and I don't want to be!

"If you are the smartest person in the room, then you are probably in the wrong room," I say to her. Think about that. Is your ego getting in the way? We then begin discussing think tanks and how vital these groups are to one's success. And, then, I have an epiphany. My dad was a member of a think tank for more than 15 years. One of the rules of this particular think tank was as follows: If a member dies, then the group appoints a committee of three to four members who come in and help the successor run his or her business. How cool is that? This was expert counsel!

It is at this moment that I realize exactly what I had done so many years ago. When the committee called to offer their help, I turned them down and resigned from the group. I told them I was not interested. Imagine that. I was so arrogant! The "expert counsel" I had needed was there all along. They wanted to help me.

But, in order to be ready to "seek expert counsel," I needed humility and I was far from that. My journey was required in order to arrive at a place where I could take advantage of that expertise.

What a great lesson I learned so many years later, sitting at my kitchen table. Keep it very, very, very humble! Thank you.

EDITOR'S NOTE

It is my opinion that one of the most fascinating aspects of self-development is in fact that there is always work to be done, that the journey is ongoing. During a quick conversation about final revisions to this story, Jim Shorkey read to me the section that has now become the epilogue. He asked me whether or not I felt it was essential to the story and I answered with, "Absolutely." I explained to him that not only was it interesting, but it contained what is called "bookends," or a reference to a significant event that was mentioned earlier in the story. I thought it was especially poignant that the conversation with his sister-in-law had happened on the day it did, a date he had explained early in his writing was the anniversary of his father's death. Here he was sharing his thoughts about his journey twenty years later on that exact day — I found it remarkable.

I heard him take a deep breath in and then he said, "Caroline, I never even thought of that. It's the day my dad died. Wow. I just — it didn't click when I wrote that."

I was shocked. I thought surely he had noticed this and considered it a happy coincidence. But he was surprised by this realization as much as I was awestruck by how we had come full circle. It was proof indeed that not only would the discoveries along this path be ongoing, but also that they would be forever available to the student who remains open to the possibility.

– Caroline Shannon-Karasik

BIO

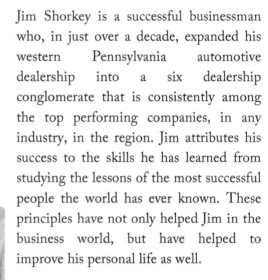

Jim Shorkey is a successful businessman who, in just over a decade, expanded his western Pennsylvania automotive dealership into a six dealership conglomerate that is consistently among the top performing companies, in any industry, in the region. Jim attributes his success to the skills he has learned from studying the lessons of the most successful people the world has ever known. These principles have not only helped Jim in the business world, but have helped to improve his personal life as well.

Jim created his newest venture, Results From Thinking, for the sole purpose of sharing the formula for success that Jim himself followed while building his automotive empire. Jim's belief is that this formula is transferrable to anyone and to any business. His informative and inspiring talks will take you through exactly what he did to turn his business from "bankruptcy imminent" to the profitable company that it is today and, through his programs, he will teach you the skills needed to reach this level of success in any area of your life. If you can tell Jim Shorkey what you want, he can show you how to get there!

To learn more, visit: www.ResultsfromThinking.com or you can email Jim directly at JimShorkey1957@gmail.com.

FOLLOW THAT VOICE TO FORTUNE
By: Diana Dentinger

We are so fine tuned to focus our attention on the outside world, to fit in, to follow in other people's footsteps and to fail, just like them, at finding happiness. Instead, what I have found, is that when you turn your attention inside, you "hear" life altering suggestions that lead you down a more fulfilling life path; one that is waiting for you to explore, if you'd just listen.

The reason I feel so compelled to share this intimate story with you is because I feel that now is the time that people are ready to add this precious quality to their other mental faculties.

What is missing if you only use thought, feelings, reasoning, will power and ethics to decide your actions? These are fine if you need to obey predefined objectives. These are fine if you want to stay within the limits of your past beliefs.

What is it though, that opens you up to limitlessness? Is there something else? Yes, there is. It is called Intuition. In my over 25 years of training and coaching, when talking about intuition, people tend to shun it, deny it or are afraid to talk about it. Yet all great people of our past and present admit the value of their intuition.

Napoleon Hill wrote "the Thirteenth Principle, known as The Sixth Sense, through which Infinite Intelligence may and will communicate voluntarily, without any effort from or demands by the individual." I use the words intuition, the "voice" and sixth sense interchangeably.

My life would be totally different if I did not listen to the "voice" of my intuition.

It is the summer of 1984 and I am walking down the street near Westminster Abbey in London with college friends. We had spent three months traveling all over Europe after graduation and this was our final destination.

"I know I have to do it, but how?" I asked myself. I had seen so many amazing places and the beauty of Florence; the excitement of Rome and the romance of Venice moved my soul profoundly. I felt so at home in those places, like I had already walked their streets before. Even when I was in Germany, there was a feeling of comfort. It was so hard to explain but one thing was for sure, I had to stay.

The next day I would be on a plane back home to the Midwest in America and my heart sunk. A "voice" told me not to go. "Diana, you belong in Europe", it said.

So I mustered up the courage to call my dad and with a pocket full of coins, I stepped into one of those famous, red phone booths on the corner adjacent to Big Ben. I still know exactly where it is. His secretary answered and she said he was in an important meeting. I told her that this was pretty important too. After a few minutes and quite a few shillings, he got on the line.

At first I thought I would ask him what he thought about me staying, but my money was running out and I only had time to say, "Dad, I am not going to be on the plane tomorrow. I am going to Germany. I want to find a job and study German."

He did not take it well. He let out a splurt of a hundred objections in only sixty seconds and when I heard the signal that the call was finishing, I said, "I will call you when I get to Germany." And the line went dead. I felt relieved. I felt confident. This was the best thing for me.

The next morning, I left my backpack and belongings at the Victoria train station on purpose, and accompanied my friends to the airport to say goodbye. I tried to get reimbursed for my ticket without any luck. Now it looked like I was not only staying but even stuck in Europe.

I took the noon train that headed south, got the hovercraft across the English Channel and arrived in Munich the next morning. What I remember most about that journey was that I felt so connected to myself. I did not feel afraid. I did not feel alone. I did not feel worried. I felt pure excitement.

What happened over the next month was quite amazing. Upon arrival in Munich, I went to the American Consulate to find out how I could get a job. They suggested I become an au pair. One woman there was so helpful and set up an interview a day for the entire next week. There were many families looking for English speaking babysitters.

But things did not go the way I imagined. None of those families really felt right. I started to get discouraged. I wondered if I really should have stayed. I questioned if my intense desire to be in Europe was right. My money was running out so I needed to get a plan B. I thought I would give it a few more days and then go find a waitressing job, maybe in the south of France.

The next day though, I got a call from the women at the Consulate. She got in touch with me through the youth hostel's phone number where I was staying. She said she thought she had the perfect family for me. Sure enough it was and I started work the same day!

They had an adorable British au pair who was returning home in another four days. During the day she showed me what chores I needed to do for the family, and in the evenings she took me out to meet people. There was quite a fun group of international people in the au pair association she belonged to. It was similar to a modern meet up or Internations group with both young men and women.

Through one of my new girlfriends there, in just a few weeks, I met the man who would become my husband. He was Italian. I had seen myself in "my dream life" living in Italy. Somehow Munich "called" me as a first stepping-stone to get where I really belonged.

So many times in our lives we get that "calling" or "flash" inviting us to do something. In that split second it is a real voice, fast yet calm, intense yet patient. It is void of fear. It is genuine. It indicates the way.

Then our mind, our ego or our rationality steps in to run the show. We start to hear another "voice". But this one is of doubt, decision and duality. We get wrapped up in a dynamic of flight or fight, pleasure or pain, right or wrong. The voice cautions us not to make mistakes.

Have you lived either of these situations before? Have you ever thought you "heard a voice"? Did you follow its suggestions? Many of my clients, and especially top entrepreneurial men, have confided in me that their intuition is what helps them make the majority of their decisions. And they add that this is something they dare not let anyone on the Board know about! Why is it then that this "all inspiring" quality, for those who know it, is kept such a secret?

Napoleon Hill writes "there is plenty of evidence to support the belief that the subconscious mind is the connecting link between the mind of man and Infinite Intelligence. It is the intermediary through which one may draw upon at will. It, alone, contains the secret process by which the mental impulses are modified and changed into their spiritual equivalent. It, alone, is the medium through which prayer may be transmitted to the source capable of answering prayer."

The "voice" came on again loud and clear when I decided I wanted to find a real job and use my Marketing degree for something more than ironing and washing floors. I spent eight fantastic months with Dr. Abel's family. Mrs. Abel and I were like sisters. She was happy to have my company during the day and I appreciated her care.

My intention was clear; it was time for a change for the better. Then out of the blue, I felt like I "needed" to take my car to the mechanics. The one they recommended was in a different part of the city. I checked out the map but could not find the street. I kept driving in circles. It was off the beaten path with no stores or homes anywhere. Then I saw a person on a corner so I stopped and asked, in German, "Entshuldigung, Wo ist Hertzig Weg?" He answered, "Ich bin Amerikaner" to which I answered, "I am American too!"

He told me he was setting up a business in a vacant building nearby and I said that I was looking for a job. He did not speak German and I did. We made great business partners. For the next three years we created an amazing array of services for the NATO soldiers, helping them find affordable apartments on the economy, buy BMW's and ship them back home when they left. We even sold insurance, airplane tickets and anything they needed.

A more profound and transformational experience with the "voice" came in the year 2004 when I was in the Paris airport on a connecting flight to Cincinnati. I was wasting time just looking around at the duty free perfumes when I was "told" to go to the restroom. Without thinking, I put down the bottle of Shalimar and walked to the ladies room.

There was one woman in line. She had dreadlocks and an incredibly beautiful amethyst stone necklace. I reached over to touch it and she said, "I'm sorry, I don't let anyone touch it. It's a healing stone." I had "asked" to meet a healer in my intentions just the week before since one of my favorite cousins, my age, had been diagnosed with cancer.

47

Sure enough she and I were on the same plane, and sure enough she lived in the same city as my cousin. She said she was "called" to be on that plane and that she left Saint Petersburg Russia a week early. Sondraya was a catalyst for many things in my life. She took me to Brazil where I met John of God, with whom I continued to work for years, even heading up his crystal bed sessions in New Zealand.

Had I not listened to that rapid-fire message while at the duty free shop, I do not know what my life would look like now. I think it might be "empty". Sure, I might have met a whole set of other interesting people. I guess I will never know. What I do know is that the times I listened things always worked out well.

As a Corporate Consultant, I am open-minded and openhearted. My clients find me very practical, but they also feel that there is something more to my coaching than what meets the eye. In Team Building Training a few years ago, a woman was complaining about the latest company policies while everyone else was sharing their wins. She got quite flustered and for some unknown reason I blurted out, "Well you would not be so worried if you could get over feeling compared to your sister."

She started crying and had a total meltdown and release of tension. Then she asked how I knew she had a sister. I answered that I did not know but that I just said what came to me in that moment.

"Every human brain is both a broadcasting and receiving station for the vibration of thought, every human brain is capable of picking up vibrations of thought which are being released by others."
-Napoleon Hill

I have learned to trust that spontaneous "transmission" of information. It's not calculated, elaborated or confabulated. It just is. And it comes unexpectedly, at the right time, in the right place for the right person. At first I let diplomacy and "I shouldn't be so straightforward" get in my way. Then the more I became comfortable with speaking from this perspective, the more other people opened up that they too perceived, sensed and intuited things.

I love my intuitive nature. I am sure I was born with it, just like everyone else, but happy I have also refined it. Over the years, the "voice" has spoken to me many times.

Sometimes it comes as a soft caress. It told me "important children will be born" the minute before I walked down the aisle to get married. It was so moving, my eyes teared up and I glanced over at my dad who was finishing his cigarette. He probably thought I was choked up for the ceremony. Thanks to this "message", I have used it as a guiding principle in my parenting. I know that subconsciously and even consciously my children know they are here for a higher purpose and to make a difference.

Other times the "voice" comes like a buddy who taps you on the shoulder to nudge you to do something. It told me "walk out of the house and take a left to start your errands" on a morning I urgently needed to find a physical therapist. And sure enough, I met one at the dry cleaners after 5 minutes. Had I turned right, I would have been at the market in an entirely different area.

Last year it was silent. I knew it was because I was pressuring myself to finish my book. Then when I stilled my mind and put away the well thought out outlines and charts, it told me "change the book into a story instead of a step by step process". With that the whole story of "Modus Vivendi" flowed through me in just over a week. My daughter was the only one I read the day-by-day excerpts to as they came to me. She shared the journey with me and even more so she shared the tears of joy for how moving this experience was for me.

Receiving information and knowledge from this infinite source moves the soul. And aren't we here as souls to have a human experience?

If your energy is only directed outwards, to the things around you, to pleasing others, to keeping up with the Joneses, you live your life through five senses. And you strive to get more and more to make you happy. Then one day, you realize that nothing external can completely fulfill you. That is the day you turn to find that more inside of yourself.

Sooner or later, all human beings ask themselves these questions: Who am I, Why am I here, What more can I be? I have found that my answers have come subtly through my intuition.

I call my "voice" an "it" because it seems to have a life of it's own, as if it were separate from me. Yet I know it is part of me. Whether it is in my heart or in my head or from some higher part of my being, it is one of the many things I feel blessed to have in life.

It has helped me feel fearless and supported in many times of trouble. Living far from home, with no relatives, raising my 4 children pretty much on my own, it has been a trusted advisor.

The "voice" has helped me stay positive and keep the faith. Even when it warned me of accidents, I was prepared for the news, the hospital stays and the loss. I feel fortunate because I have decided to worry less and trust more.

Napoleon Hill encourages us to "kill the habit of worry by reaching a general blanket decision that nothing which life has to offer is worth the price of worry. With this decision will come poise, peace of mind, and calmness of thought which will bring happiness."

Most of all, the "voice" has guided me to live my life's purpose. It has nourished my self-confidence giving me signs that confirm when I am on the right path. It has helped me continue to be an inspiration to those I serve.

My fortune has always come when I have done these three things. Intend. Intuit. Inspire. Very often you have gotten what you wanted. And at times, you have found answers and solutions through coincidences. And at other times, you got them through some kind of strange "suggestion". Even if you never told anyone else about it, you knew that something more than logic was guiding you.

Through sharing these simple stories from my life, I wish to inspire you so you deepen your connection this thing that I call the "voice". And in the silence of your inner world; listen to follow your "voice" to find your fortune.

BIO

Diana Dentinger is an innovative change maker and influential thought leader who inspires you to be yourself. "Modus Vivendi - Your Life Your Way", her number one self help, transformation book, takes you on a journey to discover how to find, name and live your potential.

Diana has been an Entrepreneur, Corporate Trainer and Executive Coach for over 25 years, certified in all the major behavior assessments. Finding them incomplete and outdated she set out to create a 21st Century performance and personality profile to catalyze long lasting change and improvement in individuals for overall personal and professional happiness.

To create this tool, Diana spent years in rigorous, scientific brain research, studying with top European Sociologists, Anthropologists and Psychologists to become a neurobiology therapist for psychosomatic illnesses.

Applying biological principles of the brain and advanced knowledge about human programming, she found the key to unlock the secrets to a meaningful life. Diana is specialized in etymology, key word coding and symbology.

She elaborated both the leading edge Personality & Needs Profile™ as well as her proprietary Coaching Programs "Modus Vivendi" and "Your Life Your Way" available as VIP In Person Intensives and Online through E-Learning.

Diana blogs about the meaning of psychosomatic illnesses and offers formulas for increasing your energy and fulfillment.

American born in Chicago, Illinois, Diana has lived over 30 years in Europe raising her 4 children in northern Italy. She loves to travel, dance, study and have fun.

Visit her at www.themeaningoflifeschool.com

DESIGN YOUR ULTIMATE LIFE
By: Andreas Jones

"Make your life a masterpiece; you only get one canvas"
-E. A. Bucchianeri

Generally, masterpiece is usually attributed to arts and crafts. It refers to a creation that has been given much praise, especially one that is considered the greatest work of a person's career, or to a work of outstanding creativity, skill, or workmanship. The word masterpiece was probably derived from the Dutch word "meesterstuk" or German "meisterstuck".

When creating your masterpiece remember what Napoleon Hill said,
"Whatever the mind can conceive and believe it will achieve."

So there is no limit to how grand your life masterpiece can be.

What makes a true masterpiece? Every moment we are creating our experience. Our thoughts, our words, our actions are all instances of our ability to bring forth something in the space where nothing existed before. Life is the canvas, our relationships are the canvas, conversations are the canvas, and dreams are the canvas. So many of us have come to believe that creativity is reserved for the select few that only some have any artistic ability and that the rest are regulated to a life of consuming and creations of others.

This is simply not true, and you don't need to look very far to see that you are a powerful creator of your reality.

Your life is a masterpiece, a beautiful work in progress that you are constantly refining and evolving as you learn new lessons and techniques for bringing forth your greatest potential and as you use your imagination to set your sights on what is possible.

It is engaging, timeless, breathtaking, original, and bold. It is relevant to the times, and it carries a message for humanity. What if your life was a movie, a book, a painting or a dance? Would do you want to be boring, unconnected or repetitive? Or would you want to create a unique masterpiece? I believe there's a higher purpose for which you were born, beyond eating, sleeping, and sexing; the most important masterpiece you'll ever create is your life. But to create your masterpiece you must first have a vision of what it looks like. Once you have a vision, which is your thought, then you can DESIGN. This leads to the process of CREATING or building according to your design. At any moment, you may need to effect some changes, this is when your ACTION reflects your innermost choice. These steps can lead you to achieving the ultimate life.

For years, it was believed that the brain was fixed and immutable-that we were stuck with what we were born with in terms of our hardware and its abilities. Then came research to show we were wrong, including Sharon Begley's book "Train your mind, Change your brain", which offered groundbreaking documentation to support the idea that we can even change our brains by changing our mental habits.

So where do we start? What needs to be changed about the way we think anyway? Let's look first at the number and nature of our thoughts. We humans, it seems, have anywhere from 12,000 to 60,000 thoughts per day. But according to some research as many as 98% of them are exactly the same as we head the day before. Talk about creatures of habit! Even more significant, 80% of our thoughts are negative. This is important of what we call the mind/body connection, psychoneuroimmunology in medical terms. You know what this is from your own experience. If you are physically tired it is hard to think clearly. On the other hand, If you have been using your mind doing mental work all day, you are likely to feel the affects physically as well.

Before you can create the perfect vision of your life masterpiece, you need to ask these questions about what your current life has been about.

• What does your life look like when you are at your healthiest, strongest, and best?
• What does your family situation look like while you are pursuing success in your work?
• What priority should drive you each day?
• What is important?
• How do you want to feel?
• What is your passion?
• What are you doing that makes you come alive?
• What are you born to do?
• What will you have wanted to accomplish?
• When you look back on your life, what do you want to be able to say about it?

Before you answer these questions, slowdown, breathe, feel your pulse and your connection to everything around you. Let the deep core of your being tell you what it needs. Let your imagination run wild. Dare to dream big. Don't settle for less than you are worth. The richer your imagination, the more beautiful your life will be. The power of imagination is incredible.

"Often we see athletes achieve on believable results and wonder how they did it. One of the

tools they use is visualization or mental imagery.
They made the choice to create their destinies and
visualized their achievements before they
ultimately succeeded.
-George Kohlrieser

See in your minds eye the life you would love to live, the person you would love to become and the relationships you would want to have. Live your life from the end and act as if all the things you need and desire are already present in your life. Feel the feelings that come from having all those wonderful things happen to you and allow those feelings to be with you at all times. As humans, we all look for meaning in life, searching consistently for an answer to questions. We want to know what the point of it all is, and how we can make our time here on earth amazingly relevant.

An important aspect towards developing good thoughts and intention is forgiveness. Forgive, release, and let go of past hurts and resentments. Feel your hearts with love. Forgive, release and let go. Not necessarily because those who mistreated you deserve it, but because you do. Let forgiveness liberate you from your past. Allow it to take away all the resentment you in your heart for all this time and allow yourself to feel in that empty space with love, inner peace and compassion. If others mistreated you in the past it does not mean you have to continue their work.

Look how beautifully Mark Twain talks about this;

"Anger is an acid that can do more harm to the
vessel in which it is stored then to anything on
which it is poured".

Release and let go of all the negativity from your life.

57

Napoleon hill said,

"Strength and growth come only through
continuous effort and struggle".

Start small and trust that as you work on letting go of all the extra baggage that is weighing you down, you will begin to feel lighter and you will gain a lot more clarity over your life. You will feel happier and more at peace with yourself and the world around you.

Through all of these, you can develop good intentions, which will lead you to visions you want to design and paint. Design is the creation or plan guiding you towards achieving your vision. It is the blueprint or template of creating your ultimate life masterpiece. There are no guarantees that life will turn out the way you want... but you have a better chance of it turning out how you want if you know how to design your own life.

I like the image of an architect designing a building by first laying out the blueprints, or a writer outlining a book starting with the table of contents. The ability to create from scratch is a powerful feeling. The house emerges from a sheet of drawings. The book takes shape from the imagination of the writer. Can you really design your own life in much the same way the architect designs the house and the writer designs a book? I do you not know if we can design every aspect of our lives because we have certain fixed and certain variable aspects? For example, we cannot change our upbringing, parents, siblings, education, childhood experiences, and all that went on before you came to this awareness of your ability to design your life. All that happened in the past has shaped who you are today, so you will need to start designing your life from this point forward.

And you can have the best-laid plans and still have them go wrong, get off track, or encounter obstacles. So since we cannot control the past and we cannot control the future, what can we control if we want to design our own life? Well, we can make a plan today, we can work our plans each day, we can modify our plan as necessary, and we can make the best of what shows up even if it is not what we want. You set out certain goals and map out a plan of action on how you will get to each one of them. Maybe you start with your ideal career and she strategized how you will get from where you are too where you want to be. Then you can design your personal life, intimate relationships, friendships, children, pets, home, hobbies, and whatever else fits in your plan. Whatever your vision looks like, your design will help you see what you need to do, in order to create your life masterpiece.

At this phase you can stop some old habits and start new ones that will lead to the realization of your vision or goal. This will require you to start a new life and you must set some standards to guide against any kind of distraction. You're ability to design your vision will help when you start the process of creation.

This is the stage at which you start to build your life according to your design. With your design in place and your mindset on success, you're ready to take the actions necessary to build your life, as you desire it. If you want to change careers, your first action may be to set up interviews with people in that career you can get guidance from. The next action may be to sign up for classes that will increase your skill level necessary for the career move. And so on. Just keep following the actions steps you outlined in your blueprint. It starts with the foundation on which you can erect your design.

Once you've nailed down what you want your life to look like, it is time to do it. The foundation is when you start small and just make minor changes to your life at first. Because of the many years of past conditioning and the intense training you have in holding on to toxic thoughts, behaviors and unhealthy relationships, given up on all that is toxic in your life will not be easy and it won't happen overnight. Chances are that you will not see major improvements in your life immediately, and that's okay. Be patient and gentle with yourself while working on rebuilding your life and remember to enjoy the journey. The point is to start making things happen, as you gain momentum, you'll begin to experience bigger and bigger changes and growth in your life, which leads to an increase in your happiness level.

It will simply lead to changes that will align your life with the vision and design you have for it. For example, you may need to exercise more and eat healthier to create your masterpiece. Or perhaps you may need to spend more time with your family because your masterpiece includes great relationships with your kids. Or you might realize that you're not spending enough time on your priorities and therefore your masterpiece is not developing like it should. Whatever your masterpiece looks like, your design will help you see what you need to do, or stop doing, and order to create it.

I also want to caution you to make sure you are building your masterpiece and not someone else's idea of what your masterpiece should be. I know this well. My mom always wanted me to be a doctor. I planned on going to medical school after college. When I was in undergrad I took a business elective class and that class changed the trajectory of my life. After taking that class I went to my adviser and switched my major to business economics. I did not tell my mom for a few semesters because I did not want to disappoint or hurt her because I was the one hurting everyday because I was suppressing my truth. My friend said that when I change my major, no one could believe it. They said it was legendary. What I think is legendary is when someone stops trying to create someone else's masterpiece and instead focuses on designing and creating the masterpiece that they are meant to build.

Make an effort and start making the life of your dreams a reality. Change is scary; this should be scary in a very good exhilarating way. Every moment we are creating our experience. Our thoughts, our words, our actions are all instances of our ability to bring forth something in the space where nothing existed before.

Always remember:

"There is one quality which one must possess to win, and that is definiteness of purpose, the knowledge of what one wants, and a burning desire to possess it".
-Napoleon Hill

BIO

Andreas is the leading authority on small business growth and profitability, #1 International Bestselling author, coach, speaker, consultant and trainer and army combat veteran. Andreas is the founder of Combat Business Coaching and the Wealthy Business Academy.

Service in the US Army forged Andreas's character. It tested him, tested his endurance, faith, and internal fortitude. He describes it as "a trial by fire" and remains profoundly grateful for it.

When he finally left the Army he did so with an astute understanding of self-ownership, implementing a vision, and the value in establishing trust and reputation. Jones applied all that he had learned serving his country to a series of jobs, including that of a VP at Sun Trust Bank. Each of his positions has endowed him with the type of knowledge required to start his own business and to provide a workable schematic for others to follow.

Andreas has taken his hard-won Army lessons into the world of business, continuing to learn new skills and insight. Each fresh challenge, project or position has helped him grow into the successful individual he is today.

In his coaching and speaking, he spotlights core concepts of leadership, integrity, and discipline. He prepares people to use these traits to execute their ideas and goals with excellence and precision. Andreas inspires his clients to live lives of significance and build legacies of influence.

Connect with Andreas at: www.andreasajones.com , Andreas@AndreasAJones.com or call at 404-376-6452

PASSING THE ROCK
By: Nigel Wall

As a multi-sport athlete there was one 'nag' in my head that simply would not go away, my fear of water, specifically my face being in water. Yes, I had done huge running races including ultra-marathons of up to 56 miles. I could cycle 100 miles in one shot without a second thought and I was also very competitive as a kayaker, but the fear of my face being in water was holding me back from my next big goal: to complete an Ironman race of 2.4 miles of swimming, a 112 mile bike ride and a 26.2 mile run.

So, I used my methodical and personally tried and tested approach to all of my goals, especially the big ones:

- Write down the goal and get really specific

- Document the 'why', the driving motivation to achieve them

- Complete an action plan with sub goals

My view of goals and obstacles is always the same: attack them head on! So I embarked on a full force approach to learning to swim propelled by my motivation to cross that line of the Ironman race.

Interestingly, I actually got to the stage of really enjoying swimming, especially in the warm Caribbean waters around where I live. Needless to say my approach worked and on the 1st of December 2013 I got to hear those awesome words "Nigel Wall from Trinidad and Tobago, you are an Ironman!"

This seems a pretty routine read so far and the reason is simple: nothing got in my way. There were no real challenges, just the habits of training, training and more training. Even on race day the swim was my strongest discipline and, other than a minor crash on my bike, the race went according to plan and I finished 6 minutes ahead of my 13-hour goal. This is not always the case, and I am not just talking about racing and athletics. In my now 60 years on this planet I have experienced many challenges as I have made progress in all areas of my life which lays the foundation for the rest of the story.

As we moved into 2014 the swimming bug had bitten and I was hooked. I was still running and riding, but swimming is a relaxing and forgiving sport and it gave me a break from the higher physical stress of the other disciplines. Like always, I was looking for challenges and I heard about this local swim, billed as one of the toughest in the region. It basically is a swim around one of the islands in the Gulf of Paria, Gasparee, here in Trinidad waters. It is a 3.5-mile course that has the same start/finish point on the north of the island. It was about a mile further than I had ever swum before but the added complication of possible big waves and strong current is what turned it from a tough swim into a monster challenge!

It looked very doable though and with massive safety and support I was not concerned too much. I upped the training and headed over to the island for the start with all the other swimmers on February 15th, 2014. I asked lots of questions of the more experienced people and while they were very supportive, they all warned of the strong head current at the north east of the island and possible big winds later on which would trigger waves. So feeling just a little nervous, I started with the first group and off we headed east, across the north of the island. Open water swimming requires 'sighting'. Maybe once every 10-15-swim strokes you pop your head up to make sure you are on the right course. Swimming off course is a big danger and you can expend huge amounts of energy getting back on course as well as moving out of the protection of the kayakers who are supporting you.

The swim progressed well as I headed over to the North East of the island in good conditions. I saw other swimmers around me so I was confident and felt strong and in the groove. There were a few light waves that were a little uncomfortable as they were coming from my left, and as a 'lefty' breather, since I breathe every other stroke on my left side, I was getting the odd mouth full of water. No stress though…it was all good.

I noticed the island to my right moving away which meant I had to gradually swim a little closer to the island as we started to turn South near the old Fort. This was where I was advised that I would feel some head-on current and maybe even headwinds and waves. Sure enough as I started to head South I felt bigger waves head-on and also noticed something strange, as I sighted the island on my right I noticed a big rock just past the Fort which didn't seem to be moving. Head back down another couple of minutes, and I look up and see the same rock in the same place. A sudden realization floods over me: the wind, waves and current are all head-on and I am not moving forward despite my strong efforts.

I decided to pull faster strokes and kick harder. I gave it maybe 5-10 minutes and then looked up. To my horror I was still seeing the same rock I had sighted much earlier. On top of which, all this energy exertion was starting to tire me out, and for a short while I was pushed backwards.

I remember in my earlier chats with the experienced swimmers, that many said they had to be pulled from the water for the same reasons I was now experiencing first hand. I looked around and saw some swimmers a little further away from the island, maybe 50 yards away. They were making slow but steady progress and that was inspiring. I realized that getting closer to the island meant experiencing a stronger current. I could overcome the current or the wind and waves but not both. It went against all my instincts to swim off the shortest line but right now I could not get past that damn rock and if I kept doing the same thing then I would be pulled from the water by the safety boats following another 20-30 minutes of exhaustion.

This is what I decided: I slowly adjusted my path, to move further left and away from the island. As I looked up I saw that I was actually going backwards at one point and the rock was 50-60 yards ahead. The lost ground was messing with me and I was overwhelmed with self-doubt. I looked at the nearby Kayak and thought about raising an arm; the universal sign for 'I'm done, come and get me'. I started talking to myself and using my well-worn affirmation 'I am a swimming monster' to push myself on. I winced at the cramp in my right calf and pulled my foot in to prevent it knotting. I just got my head down and ground away and after what seemed like an eternity, I saw the rock again. This time it was moving… backwards. I was finally passing the rock!

I was now back in the groove and swimming at the pace I had started with. My regular sighting checks showed me I was over halfway into the southern part of the Island, just a few minutes later. With just over two thirds of the 3.5 miles done, I was home free…well almost.

The old adage about the definition of insanity: doing the same thing over and over and expecting a different result, holds true. Of course, you have figured out already the message behind this story. To make progress in all areas of life, and I mean real progress, means a constant state of change: change in goals, change in behavior, change in attitude, change in what you do and how you do it, with a constant reminder to yourself of why you are doing what you are doing. In other words, what is your driving motivation?

Planning is definitely a key to success when setting goals, but you cannot always plan for every obstacle. I have to say that I am not a fan of the concept of having a plan 'B' just in case plan 'A' doesn't work. My experience is that it can take away your focus from the original plan and working flat out on the achievement of that goal using the planned methodology. I do believe that prior to taking on a goal it is worth doing a 'what is the best that can happen' exercise and then taking a look at how to improve the chances of it happening. Then doing a 'what is the worst that can happen' and mitigating the risk.

When I quit my career in IT, for example, and decided to become a leadership coach and author, I had no plan 'B'. What I did have was 6 months of savings that would cover my living expenses while I learned some new skills and sought out clients who would pay me. In the sixth month as the last mortgage payment left my bank account empty, I won a big leadership development contract with a multi-national organization. Sometimes you have to jump off the cliff and build your wings on the way down.

Your own personal 'rock' and your goal will determine your approach to dealing with potential issues. There is one element that cannot be planned for and that really is your determination and persistence to complete the goal. There are two elements to that, firstly your personal 'why'; what is your burning desire to achieve the goal. The second is just that plain hardheaded stubborn attitude that refuses to let you stop.

A personal story may help Illustrate this point beautifully. Early in 2007 I decided to run the 56-mile Comrades race in South Africa. At the time I had never run more than 35 miles in training, so there were 21 extra miles of distance that I had never run before.

On race day in June 2007 I felt great. I had trained to the schedule, was injury free and just looking forward to the race. I had my pace charts that showed me my times for each key stage of the race and I planned to execute to perfection, as I had the confidence in the advice I had been given by my fellow racers who were 'old timers' at this distance.

The start signal sounded, and I set off at my prescribed pace clocking off the distance markers, which measured a countdown in to the finish. As I approached the marker that signified 21 miles to the finish, I realized I was now in unknown territory.

I felt great in myself, but within minutes I felt a twinge in my left calf, my right hip joint felt sore, and in no time at all, I was a running wreck and my mind began playing tricks. "Well you've proved a point, you can stop now and nobody will question you"; "you've run further than anyone you know, you've done it"; "look, there are some other people who have stopped, you can stop too!"

What I started to realize was that there was only one thing that could stop me in this race and that was my mind. The minor pains had been there all along; they just got bigger because my mind told me so. It was all a conspiracy! Now that I knew what was happening the rest was easy. I started to push out the aches and pains and see the finish line with the cheering crowds. I was shouting at myself, yes, out loud, "this is a running race damn it, you cannot walk", "I came here to run and finish!"

And so it came true, 20 minutes ahead of schedule with 9 hours and 40 minutes of running and I crossed the finish line with the biggest piece of learning in my life: in most things, the only person who can stop you succeeding is yourself. I nearly talked myself out of one of the most rewarding experiences of my life.

Interestingly, I saw people just a few miles from the finish line sitting by the roadside having given up and waiting for the 'bailer' bus to pick them up. I looked at them and realized they had succumbed to the mental turmoil that happens in big endurance races. They had mentally quit, not physically. My philosophy then is the same now: pain is temporary; quitting is permanent!

Now back to the round the island swim and I am sure you want to know about the remainder of the amazing swim. How I staggered up the beach after the swim to rapturous applause from the onlookers.

Well, not all stories have a happy ending and the current, wind and waves were the least of my problems in the next part of the swim.

As I rounded the East of the island, starting the downwind part across the length of the coast of the island, I was in the groove again and my pace was good as I watched and spotted for the west most tip of that island that signaled the end of the rough water section and into the shelter of the bay for the easy swim back to the finish. The wind was building though and with it the waves. I was constantly battling for stability in the stroke as the waves were lifting me and then burying me in the white break. I noticed my guardian angel kayak paddler had been tipped over by the big seas and was been helped back upright by other paddlers. This was one of the most experienced kayakers in the country and if he had been tipped, it was bad. More and more of my energy was being sapped by simply getting enough air to breath and keeping the right way up. The waves were probably over 4 feet now. Then, almost inevitably it started: cramping in first my right, then my left calf muscle. The cramping was agonizing but the worst effect was that I had to stop swimming to push the cramp out at which point I was being overwhelmed in the big waves.

The cramping was almost certainly a result of a combination of the early strenuous activity in passing the rock and dehydration. Yes, dehydration is possible when swimming. In a clear lake the solution is easy, take an odd mouthful of lake water. In the sea it can only be fixed by carrying pouches of water or water/nutrition mixes. I had neither. Finishing was no longer an option, and even my overly persistent mind realized that my race was done.

My guardian angel was still bailing out his kayak so I moved into true survival mode. This involved a few swim strokes followed by treading water and stretching the calves while grabbing some deep breaths. I saw another kayak nearby and noticed he was shadowing me and keeping an eye on me in case I needed help.

I think in the end he made the decision for me and paddled over and had me grab the tail handle. Just as this happened my right calf cramped and

I cried out in pain. There was certainly no going on. He signaled a nearby support boat and they came over to collect me.

I was devastated. This was only my second ever "Did Not Finish" (DNF) in well over 150 races. Interestingly the other was during the kayak section of a multi-sport race where big seas pushed me towards rock and I had to be rescued.

As the powerboat came alongside and I was pulled onto the boat I saw a group of other swimmers in the boat. I was certainly not the only person who had been challenged. I found out later that all swimmers with me and behind me had to be recovered, as the conditions were so severe. I felt a little better, but I will be back.

On my goal list it is marked as 'unfinished business'. Passing the Rock was just part of this adventure. I am wiser now and I will conquer this swimming giant!

BIO

Born in England, Nigel started his numerous careers as a design engineer, but rapidly moved into the bustling Information Technology sector in the early 80's.

Although his career growth was impressive the journey was not always smooth and the pressures of the business world as well as redundancy caused Nigel to get onto a slippery slope of poor health. In the late 90's Nigel had moved up to smoking 50 cigarettes a day, taking no exercise, being overweight and working in a highly stressful environment. A visit to a Doctor when he was just 43 gave him the necessary shakeup to do a complete life transformation.

So he quit smoking and started running. In 6 months, he lost almost 50 pounds in weight, ran a half marathon and completely rethought his life. In 2001 he made a life changing decision to get out of the IT sector and start his own business in the area of leadership development and personal coaching.

The rest, as they say, is history. Nigel is now a recognized leader is his field, has numerous articles and a major book, Ask Leadership, in print. He is also a personal fitness coach, an Ironman Triathlete, ultra marathoner, he ran 101 miles on his 59th birthday and cycled 300 miles in one ride the year before! He also has a passion for travel and adventure and has to date travelled to 43 countries. He is an author, qualified glider pilot, sailor, accomplished musician, photographer and recently celebrated his 60th birthday by Paragliding at 10,000ft in the Andes mountains in Colombia.

PERSISTENCE AND FAITH: AN UNBEATABLE COMBINATION

By: Paul Guyon

In memory of my mother: Mary Ann Guyon. Mom Passed away before she could see this book published. I am forever grateful for her prayers, love and encouragement,

October 22, 2004. Dave the CEO, the woman from Human Resources and a tall, serious looking man arrived at my office door. It was about 3:00 O'clock in the afternoon. Dave said the tall man was with corporate security. DSI didn't have corporate security so I knew it was going to be bad news.

Dave sat down next to me and explained that my position had been eliminated. Then, to my horror, the HR woman recited the terms of my release and that I had 30 days to accept the terms to receive my severance pay. I was given a box, packed up a few things from my desk and office, grabbed my jacket and, in a numb stupor, I left DSI for good as the tall man from corporate security escorted me and my box of memories to the parking lot.

I was in shock! How could they eliminate my position? I had been a key part of the team that built DSI from zero to $53M in 14 years. In my role as Chief Information Officer, I had designed and built, from the ground up, the technology and systems that operated the company. LogiTRACK™ was our secret sauce. How could they possibly continue to function without my technology leadership into the future?

You Lost My Bag!

The biggest jump in revenue was from an innovative program that managed the delivery of "separated bags" for all of the major airlines. If you travel frequently, more than likely, you have made a trip to the airline baggage service office to report your "Lost Luggage" and your bag was delivered by one of our vendors.

The airlines prefer to use the more friendly term, "Separated" because, in reality, your luggage was probably not lost, it has merely been separated from your flight due to weather, missed transfer, or last minute schedule changes usually made by the customer. Your bag is probably enroute to your destination on a different flight, at a different time. However, by ruling of the Federal Aviation Administration the airlines are required by law to reunite you and your bag, at no cost to you, as soon as possible.

Before our Baggage Delivery Management Program came along, the airlines would contract with a local mom and pop courier service to deliver the bags. One airline reported that it processed hundreds of invoices from more than 400 bag delivery vendors across their entire North American network at a cost of $38 per invoice, each week!

Because of the sheer volume, thousands of invoices were simply rubber stamped and approved for payment. The invoices were eventually paid in 30-90 days. There was no proof of delivery, no audit to insure the correct amount was billed, and most importantly, there was no way to control how the representative of the airline, the baggage delivery vendor, treated their valuable customer.

The Baggage Delivery Management program solved all of these problems, and also saved the airlines millions of dollars, and helped improve customer service and brand loyalty. Every two weeks, we would present the airline with a single electronic invoice for their entire network, completely audited, with proof of delivery, by uniformed, professional looking, insured drivers.

The entire invoice audit, online proof of delivery, and payment process was completely paperless. By the time I left DSI in 2004, this innovative program was generating about $40M in gross revenue!

How It All Began: Cradle Catholic

Born March 5, 1958 the fifth son of Drs Joseph and Mary Ann Guyon at St Joseph Hospital in Flint, Michigan, baptized March 23, 1958, first communion in the 2nd grade. I have four brothers, David, Greg, Richard, Mark and later, Ann Marie who was born when I was eight.

My brothers and I went to church every day before school at St Francis of Assisi. Mom and dad were devout Catholics and we went to Mass as a family every Sunday in our Sunday best. My brothers and I were altar boys as well.

Corporal Punishment, Dial Soap and the Self-Made Man

My father used the belt; the Guyon boys were an unruly bunch and we received the belt whenever we really crossed the line. I remember we tried to withstand the belt by tucking an Etch-a-Sketch in our pants when we knew a whipping was coming. You can imagine how effective that was, and how my dad responded with even more vigor!

Being the youngest boy, I mimicked my brothers and quickly learned to swear, or cuss, as we used to call it. But, instead of a single swear word, I would string all the words together in a cussing tirade; it was a glorious sonnet of vulgarity! When mom heard my shameful cussing, I learned the taste of Dial soap! I cannot stand the smell (or taste) of Dial soap to this day!

Dad had two open-heart surgeries and a stroke by the time I started school. I remember taking walks with him to rehabilitate; I loved my dad, especially during those walks. He would hold my hand as we walked and told me not to go too fast, because he could not keep up. Through no fault of his own, Dad's illness turned him into an absentee dad, he tired easily and sought a new specialty in medicine that was not as demanding as family practice. Eventually, his absence and how I dealt with it nearly cost me everything.

While my father was busy pursuing his new career, I came to idolize our next-door neighbor, Mr. Seder, instead of my absentee-dad. Jim Seder was an entrepreneur; had his own business, was successful, was a pilot and rode a motorcycle, all without ever going to college – mom said he was a self-made-man – I decided I would become a self-made-man too; I was five years old. I have pursued the entrepreneurial dream ever since then.

Castaways on the Island and my Fall from Grace

Dad's new job brought the family to our new home on Grosse Ile, a large island at the junction of the Detroit River and Lake Erie. It was 1966 and I was entering third grade, at Sacred Heart Catholic School. Feeling like a fish out of water in my new school, I tried desperately to fit in.

Sacred Heart closed after the seventh grade and I chose to attend Grosse Ile Junior High School instead of continuing my Catholic education. This is where I discovered the temptations of sex, drugs and rock-n-roll. I have been a drummer and musician all of my life, and for the first time, I was in a real rock-n-roll band and had the opportunity to pursue the dark side of life. I boarded the train of self-worship and pleasure seeking that would dominate the course of my life for the next 38 years. My idol quickly became the quest for pleasure. My relationship with my father deteriorated over the next 10 years. He said I was a hedonist, he was right.

I graduated from Grosse Ile High School in 1976 and was already spending time in the bars since the drinking age had changed from 21 to 18.

75

Later, when the drinking age changed back to 21, I was briefly underage but it didn't matter; the local bartenders knew me and never asked me for my ID.

I got my first steady job in a local aluminum siding factory and started making a decent living. It was hard work so we drank and partied every night and got up early the next day to do it all over again. I was making good money and life appeared to be great but deep down I was not happy. I continued my hedonistic ways; medicating with drugs and alcohol. Something was missing. As for my faith in God, it went out the window.

My First Exposure to Personal Development

Once I left my job at the aluminum factory, I started playing music again while also looking for a job. It was 1980 and the IBM Personal Computer had just hit the market. My dad told me I should get into either computers or management.

I could have gone to a university, but being the aspiring entrepreneur, self-made-man I was, I sought the shortest route to get a computer job so I went to tech school and got a certificate. I landed a job as a computer salesperson and consultant at a local computer store. I learned everything I could about technology, and sales and marketing. We eventually sold medical and dental office systems with much success. I excelled at the implementation and design of systems and marketing.

In my role in sales and marketing, I studied and applied everything I had learned to our business. I kept searching for growth and another angle to get ahead. I joined an MLM called Shaklee and listened to a ton of motivational material, I was hooked! I learned there was hope and the possibility to succeed as an entrepreneur seemed more real than ever. I kept reading, learning and seeking.

A Hole in my Heart

My father died in June of 1985 and I felt lost and empty. After a string of failed relationships, I decided it was time to marry because I thought it would help fill the hole from his loss. I married Rhonda in September of 1985. On my wedding day, I told Rhonda's brother Robert if the marriage did not work out we would just get divorced.

October 6, 1986, we moved to Traverse City, Michigan. I received an offer for a promising position as sales manager for a small, startup computer consulting company. Truthfully, in addition to the great opportunity, I moved to get away from the bad influences, and the bridges that I burned with family and friends. Even though I escaped the influences of the big city, I soon realized it was very easy to drink and smoke pot. I joined a band and started gigging regularly, drinking and drugging on the weekend.

Eventually, Rhonda and I grew apart and were divorced in 1992. It was entirely my fault. I needed to grow up. (I recently approached Rhonda through her brother Robert and apologized to her and her family for my selfishness.)

In 1991, I got a great new job as the IT manager at DSI, and fell in love with a new woman named Leslie the following year. Rhonda and I were already finished by then. I celebrated my divorce at a local pub by getting a DUI and a serious reality check from God. The Judge ordered me to quit drinking, attend weekly Alcoholics Anonymous meetings and go to group counseling.

AA and group counseling were very helpful, it improved my outlook, and I looked at my life in a new light. In my final interview, my counselor told me that I was not an alcoholic, but advised if I were ever in a similar situation that I should seek help. My sobriety was short lived; it lasted about 11 months.

A Growing Family and Career

My new job as Chief Information Officer at DSI was really taking off and Leslie and I bought a house together and started a family. I continued to party and play music. We were married in March of 1996 and our first of three beautiful sons, Jacob, was born in August of 1996, he is a very sensitive and kind young man.

The rules of the game of life had once again changed, as I had a new life and wife to take care of and the responsibilities of a growing family. The pressure of these new responsibilities carried over into my job. Stress at home and work increased and unfortunately, my partying escalated. I was making good money at this point and climbing the corporate ladder.

Our second son, Joseph, was born in August of 2000; I named him after my father. At six feet five, he is quite the athlete with his basketball career taking off! Elijah was born in April of 2003. He'll probably become a self-made engineer, blacksmith or survivalist with his own reality TV show someday. I just love watching Jacob, Joseph and Elijah grow into manhood.

After I lost my job at DSI, I also lost myself. Once again, my selfishness and hedonistic ways ruined my marriage to Leslie; she made a valiant effort to save our marriage but I did not cooperate. In reality, I was not ready to leave my wretched life. Finally, in 2006, she took the kids and left me. We were divorced in 2008.

As you might expect, the divorce had a profound and negative effect on my three sons. Jacob and I had been two peas in a pod... now Jacob hated me and would not spend time with me during visitation. We are still repairing our relationship to this day. So at this point, I lost the job of a lifetime, my marriage, my sons, and even my faith in God.

I had lost my way — I was devastated.

A New Lease on Life

As my life continued to spiral out of control, I found myself in a caustic relationship with a woman, to protect her identity, I'll call her Missy. She helped me learn a big lesson, and I am forever grateful, because she also liked to drink like me. She totally turned me off to drinking and partying, as she was also abusive when she drank. She kicked me out of the house on Labor Day weekend, 2008, and I proceeded to go on a 3-day drinking binge. It was then that I finally hit rock bottom and said; "Enough is enough!"

I have not had a drink ever since!

Coming to My Senses – My New Purpose in Life

I knew I had to get away from Missy. I wanted, more than ever, to get back to my sons and possibly reconcile with Leslie, or at least make things right between us and be a more present and dedicated father.

I had finally discovered my purpose in life; to become the best father and man I could possibly be. I made an exit strategy to leave Missy, got sober, saved some money and moved out a year later in 2009.

Sage Advice from a Pediatric Heart Surgeon from India

After leaving DSI, I turned to Internet Marketing to supplement my income. I joined Willie Crawford's Internet Marketing Inner Circle to learn from the best. This was my first exposure to Napoleon Hill and the book, Think and Grow Rich. I was about to discover one of Napoleon Hill's, and life's most important concepts, your definite purpose.

One member of the inner circle was always giving value first; his name was Dr. Mani Sivasubramanian, Dr. Mani for short. Dr. Mani called himself an Infopreneur; expertly applying information marketing to fund life saving heart operations for children in India born with congenital heart disease whose families could not afford them. These children would likely perish without surgery.

Dr. Mani once told me; "Paul, why don't you stop focusing on yourself and focus on helping others instead?" That seemingly insignificant piece of advice launched a new beginning for me and spawned the first step towards discovering my purpose in life and the idea for my first information product.

In December of 2008, I launched my first information product. It was called the Food to the Rescue Cookbook. It featured the favorite recipes of area celebrities, chefs and people in the community. Not only was the cookbook a success it also raised awareness and publicity for Food Rescue of Northwest Michigan. Today the food rescue operation has recovered over 6 million pounds of fresh food. That's over 6 million meals in 7 years!

I had finally learned that helping others was far more important than helping myself. In helping others I have found my blessings too numerous to count.

Faith: My Personal Key to Success

In September of 2009, I met Dana Pratt III for a business lunch. However, the business part of the discussion was short as we talked about my new life. He said he had a feeling our meeting was not to discuss business, but instead, it was to invite me to join a Christian men's group called Men's Fraternity.

Men's Fraternity was the first experience EVER of living my faith at home and at work! I was seeking to find a way to repair the damage I had done to my relationships with my sons, especially with Jacob. Men's Fraternity was a key step towards healing with Jacob and the genesis of my faith journey that continues to this day.

I learned that we can only rely on ourselves for the will or desire to accomplish a thing, but it requires trust in a higher power, trust in God, and the action of the Holy Spirit to reach our goal. We can do nothing worthwhile without God.

My Journey Home

Wrapping up my story of transformation would not be complete without telling you of my journey back to the Catholic Church. One day, I got in the car and Catholic Radio was playing. I wondered how that happened. I am positive the Holy Spirit caused the station to turn from the Rock Station WKLT to EWTN. I immediately was hooked on Catholic Radio and listened to nothing else for the next year.

On December 24, 2012 I decided I should go to midnight Mass. An hour before Mass, I marched up to Fr. Greg's residence over at St. Patrick's Catholic Church and rang the doorbell, he came to the door with the telephone to his ear. He was making final arrangements with his family for the Christmas Holiday. I said; "I need to see you before Mass!" he responded as every good pastor would; "Surely you've had every opportunity to go to confession during Advent." He had no idea I had not been to confession in 38 years. I repeated myself; "I need to see you before Mass!" He agreed.

I almost walked away, but said to myself as I walked into church, "No, you are going to HAVE to hear my confession today!" Moments later, I confessed a lifetime of sin; through Fr. Greg, Jesus forgave my sins and told me to go in peace and sin no more! The massive weight of guilt and shame I was carrying for the past 38 years finally lifted from my shoulders. I was free for the first time in my life!

A Brand New Life

To say I have turned a new leaf is an understatement. I no longer talk to some of my friends at all. When I do see them, the conversation is cordial. We have nothing in common, except our past. Since my conversion, I attend church regularly. I am very involved; as a reader of the Gospel and member of the choir and volunteer.

Mom was thrilled with my transformation. Over the past few years, I have called her every few days and visited her more often; getting to know her better and sharing our faith. She told me she had been praying for my return to the faith all of these years. I am forever grateful she never gave up on me. Mom passed away at the age of 90 on Father's Day, 2016. I will miss her smile and her motherly touch.

God bless you Mom!

In addition to my newfound faith, I have made several significant life changes. I dropped 40 pounds in 18 months. I exercise regularly and am very active in my community. In 2013, my friend and mentor, Tony Rubleski and I hosted the Think and Grow Rich Summit, celebrating the teachings of the great Napoleon Hill and the 75TH anniversary of Think and Grow Rich.

Since hosting the Think and Grow Rich Summit, we launched a coaching and consulting practice called The Ultimate Mastermind Group. We teach and coach small business owners and entrepreneurs how to grow and build their businesses with smart marketing and technology. The part of the program I enjoy the most is helping my clients stay focused and holding them accountable to what it takes to reach their dreams and aspirations.

Bitter Turned Better

At first, I was very bitter about losing my job at DSI. I was making really great money, but I was not really happy. It took quite a while to realize money; status and possessions do not equal happiness, at least not for me. The stress of my old job was killing me, I started making mistakes, we had a major failure that caused a partial service outage. The entire organization rallied to recover and we did restore service after three painful days.

My team was stressed out too. We worked around the clock to deliver services to a fast growing organization that seriously needed re-tooling and was not in a position to slow down. In the quest for growth we had outgrown our innocence as a small, family-owned company that I loved. It was time for a change and I am grateful I was set free to pursue a better life.

Five Life Lessons Learned from my Journey to Success

1. Focus on helping others first, instead of focusing on yourself.

2. It's never too late to change your ways and turn your back on a life that does not serve you.

3. Find your big reason why. Napoleon Hill calls this Definiteness of Purpose. My purpose is to be the best possible Christian, father, businessperson, musician and friend. My dedication and focus is on raising my sons and being present for them in the best way possible. You need a good reason never to quit.

4. Be persistent. Set goals, review them daily, and make course corrections along the way. Make a plan and follow it. Never ever, give up.

5. Structure, discipline and accountability. Restructure your life and your day. Be careful of your associations, especially negative influences. Seek out a mentor, coach and/or accountability partner. Make your goals known publicly so your coach, family and friends can hold you accountable.

In Conclusion

At 58 years old, I'm just getting started with my new life as a father, former spouse, coach and believer. I've learned that self-reliance will get you pointed in the right direction. Personal development, especially the teachings of Napoleon Hill and Think and Grow Rich will serve you well as a formula for success. This formula, combined with a strong purpose, persistence and faith in God are an unbeatable combination!

BIO

Paul Guyon is the former Chief Information Officer of international logistics firm, DSI. He teaches small business owners how to create and implement systems and technology that enables ordinary people to produce extraordinary results. Mr. Guyon's clients have managed up to $40 million in business with a department of just five people.

He invented the technology to enable a new market category that streamlines the delivery, invoicing and payment of lost bags for Delta, Northwest, American and United Airlines, saving the airlines millions of potential lost customers whose precious luggage was 'separated' from them. Paul's delivery management systems saved millions of dollars for pharmaceutical giants; Pfizer, Merck and Eli Lilly.

Today Mr. Guyon teaches small business owners and entrepreneurs how to grow and build their businesses with smart marketing and technology; keeping their faith and core values at the center of their growth and lives.

Guyon makes his home in Traverse City, Michigan and enjoys an active, healthy lifestyle with his three sons. He has a passion for business, music, drumming, community service and his faith in God. Guyon says, "Any day I get to spend with my sons is a good day!"

To connect with Paul, visit his website; www.PaulGuyon.com

PERFECTLY ON PURPOSE
By: Sophia Bailey

Making sense of life when you feel less than perfect...

Firstly, I am not perfect and my life has not been perfect; my journey to success was not perfect either but my journey, my life and my Self have manifested perfectly. Sometimes it is difficult to see the reason behind life's circumstances and if you have had a difficult life, you may be embarrassed by moments in your past, as I have been. This chapter is about it being time to let go of the same of having failed and to embrace the joy in who you've become.

> *"Adversity will do something to you or for you."*
> -Napoleon Hill

The moment I discovered I was too weak to make a difference.

My Dad used to hit my Mum. I will always recall one particularly violent evening. I was 10 years old. He was unhappy that she had invited the wrong photographer to my sister's birthday party and caused a big scene so we had to leave. Downstairs, outside the building, he pushed her onto the spiked fence. The railings stuck into her breast and she screamed. I tried to pull him off. I hung on to his waist and pulled desperately kicking his legs to try to cause him enough pain to let go but I was not strong enough. That is what I told myself, "you are weak you are not strong enough". I couldn't protect my Mother, the most important person in my life and right then, right there, I had formed the second thought in life that would shape my character and my purpose.

When my Mother finally left my father, she was determined to give us the best possible start in life. Luckily for me, personal development was a part of that. We had a tin can of positive quotes that said 'success comes in cans not cannots' that I would often tip out and memorize; she helped me believe that I was special and I had a purpose in life. As far as education went, I excelled, I was bright and observant but that could not protect me for the life ahead.

"Your only limitation is the one you set up in your own mind!"
-Napoleon Hill

The moment I learned my life was a mistake.

My daughter was 6 months old when I christened her. When one of my church elders learned I was had become a Mother at the age of 17, she supportively commented, 'never mind, you have made a mistake now but you still have the rest of your life'. Somehow the words were lost in translation and what I heard was your life and your baby is mistakes.

Always be careful of the seeds you sow into the minds of the young, you may be helping them to plant or justify a negative self-belief.

I wanted to not be a mistake so I held onto abusive relationships, trying to prove that I could make it work but choosing the wrong type of person to make it work with. My child's father told me I was no longer attractive because of the weight I gained after having a baby. He decided to move on. I sat on the floor when he said he was leaving, hung tight onto his leg and bawled, I didn't know what to do to make him stay. I reminded myself that I was not strong enough to make any difference. I let him go and in that instant I was a single teenage mother.

When my mother remarried and left the country a year later, negative self-talk replayed in my mind and lowered my self-esteem. I tried to create a stable family unit but no relationship was better than the last. I didn't know what a loving relationship was supposed to look like and I accepted poor treatment because although I knew I was worth more, I was scared to defend myself. I was limited by the thought that I was weak and acted in line with that belief. My only strength came from the natural instinct to raise my daughter to be better than me.

"Faith removes limitations!"
-Napoleon Hill

The moment I decided to succeed despite the odds.

There are rules about how old you ought to be before you have your first child. Some rules are bound to be broken. Being a single mother in my teens, at a stage where I was so vulnerable, was a great learning experience. I lived on the fourth floor of a council estate with no lift; neighbors were drug dealers, drunks and addicts. Climbing up eight flights of stairs with a stroller, my bags and a baby in my arms made me physically stronger but my surroundings did nothing to strengthen my mind. Something in my spirit still whispered to me that I was special and different but at times it was difficult to believe.

On the advice of my mother, I enrolled at a local college and there I met the soon to be father of my second child. I found work in a department store and it was okay but this was not the life that had been destined to me. At age 21, I had a second daughter and returned to work when she was six months old. Picking up my girls from after school care was a struggle; I always seemed to be rushing or late, I packed the wrong lunches, my children forgot their kit and permission slips, there is no organized parenting 101 class for school leavers. Other families seemed to have it all together; I wanted that.

One day in the playground after school, my daughter cried, "I just want to be in a normal family" she knew that I was different to the older parents and wanted me to fit in. I knew that despite everything that made life seem so hard, I had to get myself together.

"Desire backed by faith knows no such word as impossible."
-Napoleon Hill

Over the next few years I borrowed accounting textbooks to study as I could not the afford university. Every summer, I sat the exams to learn a profession so I could fit in with what society expected of me. Chance gave me the opportunity to become a freelance computerized accounting specialist and I worked long and hard to prove myself in business. I quickly gained new clients and opportunities but in the process, I saw more of the office and less of my girls.

By the time I was 25, my relationship had been volatile so it didn't last and I focused on my career. I developed a new belief. I may have been weak, I may have made mistakes but my children's only fault was to be born to a young mother and if I work hard enough, I can still give them a good life. I resolved to get my life together by the age of 30. I would own my house, get a car and prove that my past was no prediction of my future. These material possessions were the measures of success that could show the world my value. I had a clear vision and I was going to have it all.

The moment I realized that time was more important than money.

That vision of success burned in me like an obsession. I was last at the office every day, got salary bonuses every year and justified the quality time lost with the quality of life I was able to afford. I got a mortgage on my house and had fun looking through catalogues with the girls to mark out pictures of the items that would be ours. The freedom of having money and choices felt good.

When the quest for material possessions is your main goal, at some point something has to give and for me this moment came one autumn evening on 2002, in the shape of a life changing phone call.

The caller let me know that the children's father had been found dead. He was 26 years old. No warning, no explanation, he simply went to bed one day and didn't wake up. I cried from shock, for the children who would grow up without their father, and for myself, knowing that I would be a lone parent once again and scared that I wouldn't cope. It was a selfish reaction, but the truthful and the deepest sadness was that someone with so many dreams would never live to carry them out. If life could end at any time, then I wondered what was I doing with my life.

It was weeks before I went back to work, suddenly exchanging all my time for money didn't seem like a worthy goal. I grew to resent my time there more every day and I longed for a way out of my job.

My childhood friend Kevin had been travelling the world having amazing experiences so I called on him for advice. It was a short powerful conversation.

Me: "How do you manage to achieve so many experiences in your life?"

Him: "Sophia, you just focus on the outcome and everything will come together for you." His answer was the first key to the success I went on to achieve and I will always be grateful.

I focused on creating happy childhood memories for my daughters and for the next few years we did just that.

> *"If you do not conquer self, you will be conquered by self."*
> -Napoleon Hill

The moment I got the courage to transform my life.

When you are clear about what you want, the opportunities to attain it show up frequently and visibly. In my search for a way out, I started a home-based business and was introduced to a personal development seminar that could help me discover new possibilities for my life.

I attended on a Wednesday evening after work; the middle of the room was packed with spaces at the front and the back. I took my seat at the front center of the room and followed along in my workbook as we figured out what wasn't working and why.

What wasn't working out in my life? My work. I wanted my time back.

What was stopping me? Fear.

Who did I need to be before I could achieve my goal? A stronger person who believed I could do it.

I wrote down the words 'courage and faith' in my workbook, the qualities I had never believed I possessed were standing between my new life and me.

When the speaker asked if anyone wanted to share, I felt like everyone else in the room, terrified to volunteer. That would mean I had to share my fears in front of a room of strangers. As I put my head down so they wouldn't pick me, the word 'courage' stared back at me from my page and even though I was afraid, I raised my hand. It was now or never. With my head still down I heard, 'Sophia, would you like to share?' I was shaking when I took a couple of steps to turn around and face the room.

As I shared my story, declared that from that point I would have 'courage and unlimited faith in my own abilities', it was as if I felt my old self leave- the energy shifted. People clapped, and I felt strong for the first time in years.

On the way home, I devised a plan. I would save up enough to leave my job and focus on running my own business full time in the next six months. What happened next was nothing short of miraculous...

I woke up feeling different, more positive. I went to work happy because I had a plan. I switched on my computer and the first email was a request to meet with the MD later that afternoon; it was strange as usually he would just pop his head around the door but given my miserable mood of late, I could understand why he hadn't.

That Thursday afternoon, I attended the meeting. When the MD told me they were making some cuts and had an offer for me, I smiled. He said 'Sophia, I know it is a long time since you spent time with your girls and you are quite entrepreneurial so as you have worked here a long time I want to give you an offer. You could change from finance to the sales department or take six months upfront pay and agree to voluntary redundancy." I told him about the seminar, chose the latter, and just like that, I was free.

"No one ever is defeated until defeat has been accepted as a reality."
-Napoleon Hill

The moment I lost the battle and won the war.

So the offer was a dream but the reality was a nightmare. It took around nine months before it had gone totally downhill.

I made bad business decisions because I'd failed to make a realistic plan.

I didn't understand my customers so I created the wrong product.

I invested unwisely in marketing without testing my message.

I got advice and help from people that weren't experts.

The list goes on but the outcome was, I was in a desperate situation, my funds were depleted. Sadly, I was not making any money and I could not afford to pay my bills. Including my mortgage.

I sat alone in the dark with the curtains closed on the day my mortgage case was in court knowing full well that they were about to repossess my house. There was nothing left. Who was I to think I could be somebody special? I told myself this never would have happened if I had kept my job. I had put myself out there and failed. Now everyone would know about it. How could I admit that I'd got it all wrong?

In the midst of it all, I got a phone call from my friend Anietie. As I explained why I would be off the radar for a while, he refused to accept my sob story and asked me a question that gave me a new perspective.

"Sophia, have you ever met a successful person who never failed or a winner that had never lost?"

I saw then, that if I tried instead of quitting, this could be just a moment in my success journey. I was not destined to fail; all I had to do was try.

One of the hardest things in my life was to let go of my ego and in the depths of my humility ask for help. I called around for money to save my home and within the next half an hour I was faxing the courts with proof of payment. I had been blessed this time, I had opened my eyes and realized there was more to being an entrepreneur than starting a business, and you had to persist.

"You can succeed best and quickest by helping others to succeed."
-Napoleon Hill

The moment I became the 1%.

My new perspective on failure being part of my journey to success kept me growing and learning. It was at this point that I got the opportunity to learn about wealth creation, sales and marketing from some of the world's wealthiest people. I applied what I was learning to my life and used my stories to help others. I grew from strength to strength as a mentor and inspirational speaker.

My children were older and had their own dreams of success. When my daughter told me that she wanted to go to university, my income was nowhere near what she needed. Getting a university loan was an option but I knew most students repaid loans for decades and after my experience with debt, it was the last thing I wanted for her. I had learned enough to know that I could do it if I focused on the outcome and persisted through the challenges.

I asked her to do three things.

1. Let me know exactly the amount you need to the nearest penny, include every detail.

2. Do not apply for any loans. We will not fail so we do not need a backup plan.

3. Have faith in the vision that when I transfer you this money, it will not be a struggle it will be so easily and effortless it will feel like pocket money.

I'd never saved up as much as 10,000 pounds in a year before but if I could help enough people achieve their goals, I could achieve mine. I started a new home-based business and this time every time I hit a challenge I found a way to solve it and persist. 80% of people that started with me, left along the way but that was not an option for me. If I quit, then my daughter would not be able to go to university and I could not live with that.

Using my life as a lesson, I shared that all I wanted was to give my children a better a life and people just like me all over the world said, 'me too'. Over the next 12 months, I had built an organization of over 7,000 people and trained thousands more. My team made over 1 million dollars in revenue for the company. I used what I knew about computerized systems, sales and marketing to help people achieve 4 and 5 figure monthly incomes, I travelled to different countries every month, sometimes taking the girls with me, but the very best moment was when I hit 'send' on the bank transfer that paid for my daughters' education in full without it making a dent in my finances, just as I had promised.

"Happiness is found in doing, not merely possessing."
-Napoleon Hill

The moment I realized what success meant to me.

My reputation grew in the stories of people I'd helped and this attracted an opportunity to work with millionaires that use direct sales as a vehicle for lasting change. The way they thought and spoke inspired me to learn more so I flew to Florida to find out more about their company, Organo Gold.

There were thousands of people at the convention and the last few years had taught me what goes on at the front of a conference room so although I attended as a VIP, I chose to sit at the back and check if all I heard was true.

For the first time, I saw people share the pain of the journey, not just the bling of their success. They really cared about everyone in the room. At a training event, I heard the head of the Napoleon Hill Foundation talked about the mission for every OG partner to read the book Think and Grow Rich and mentor one person from an adverse background so they could understand how by changing their thoughts could change their life. I had found my home.

When my company owners heard that I had partnered with OG they closed my back office and stopped my check, without notice. The industry rarely allows you to work in two businesses at once, no matter your contribution. They were trying to stop me and with my old mindset, they would have done. Instead they motivated me to work even harder at my new company, in the first month my team of business owners did over £40,000 worth of sales.

Over time, more people head hunted/sought me out for mentorship. I wanted to help people grow regardless of the industry they were in. This felt like the direction and the right time to building a legacy of wealth creators in my own right and the key was to work harder on myself than my business.

*"The way of success is the way of continuous
pursuit of knowledge."*
-Napoleon Hill

The moment I discovered how to Think and Grow Rich

I had heard that on average a wealthy creator has read the book Think and Grow Rich at least 14 times, I had read it a few times but knew there was more to understand. Studying this book would be the perfect start to my life mission. I committed myself to studying each of the thirteen steps to riches, one each month and for over a year I did nothing else.

It was during the fifth step, "Imagination" that I got my 'POP' moment. I understood the secret I had unknowingly been partner to my whole life. Looking back at my life, I noted seven lessons that I had followed over and over again to achieve success, first in my career, then in my businesses. I also noticed that when I had not followed those seven steps, I had failed to succeed. This was a formula I could pass on to others and I named it The Vision Creation Experience.

At the end of my 15 month mental cleanse, I found I could manifest my ideal outcomes in short spaces of time and by finding my flow, I saw my life was unfolding perfectly on purpose. Since then, I have become a multi award winning Wealth Creation Mentor and my seven lessons have impacted the lives of brilliant entrepreneurs from all over the world and from all walks of life.

Sharing these moments has been a healing journey for me. it was not the chapter I planned to write but I know this is the story that God wanted me to share. The thought of being able to help just one person seek answers about their purpose, motivates me to get past myself so I can impact others.

> *"Every adversity, every failure, every heartache carries with it the seed of an equal or greater benefit."*
> -Napoleon Hill

The moments that became my message.

If I had not convinced myself that I was weak and if I had grown up in a more stable family, would I have been strong enough to walk away from abusive relationships?

If I had not chosen the wrong relationships, would I have become a mother so young?

If I had not been a young mother under such adverse conditions, would I have had such a strong desire to work for a better life?

If I were not working so hard for a better life for my children, would I have discovered how much more important it was to work for quality time rather than quantity of material possessions?

If I were not seeking a way to get my time back, would I have been as driven to become an entrepreneur and attending that life-changing seminar?

If I had not been driven to become successful as an entrepreneur, would I have had the courage to continue after the first time I failed?

If I had not understood the blessing in failure, would I have persisted through every challenge until I could achieve success?

If I had not achieved success, would I have been noticed and given the opportunity to partner with millionaires?

If I had not partnered with millionaires; would I have been introduced to the Napoleon Hill Foundation and understood the true power of mentoring?

If I had not become an award winning Wealth Creation Mentor, would I be writing this message to you now?

If I were not writing this message to you now, what would be different... you tell me?

Life is perfect when you are mindful of the moments.

If you have read this entire chapter, I thank you so much for being part of my journey. I want to leave the 'POP' moment from my Think and Grow Rich study to help you make sense of life, when you feel less than perfect so I have created a short video message and online guide for you. To read it or to share your 'POP' moments visit www.PerfectlyOnPurpose.com

BIO

Mother to Genéa and Cleopatra, fiancé to Digital Marketing Expert Rune J Larsen and under the complete control of Lucy-BeLLA (HER CAT).

Sophia is a Wealth Creation Mentor that helps Brilliant Entrepreneurs turn their ideas into streams of income so they can make a bigger impact with their message. She is listed in Ninety Nine magazine as one of six of the most influential people in Black Britain, recognised by the NOI for her valuable contribution to business and wealth creation and included among the most influential and inspirational black business owners in Britain today by be mogul.

The name Sophia Bailey, when translated means Sophos Baiulus, literally meaning 'Wisdom Messenger'. Sophia says, "Wisdom is when you let go of the pain and retain the lesson". She believes that everything she has been through was in order to overcome, find the lesson and share it with others. She says, "You name it, I've been through it, learning the lessons the hard way, but learning them nevertheless. Now I understand my past was a passage to who I have become, a messenger of life's wisdom.

This chapter takes you moment by moment along her journey to success. She hopes that by reading it you are lead to seek the perfection in your own life regardless of the challenges you may have faced.

To access the free bonus video and online guide that accompany this chapter visit www.PerfectlyOnPurpose.com

AWAKENING TO SPECIALIZED KNOWLEDGE

By: Norma Edmond

"The only limitation is that which one sets up in one's own mind."
-Napoleon Hill, Think and Grow Rich.

Chapter 5, SPECIALIZED KNOWLEDGE

Personal Experiences or Observations

The 4th Step toward Riches

Around the age of four, the normal process of growth and development for a child changed dramatically for me. Imagine being less than 5 years of age and being forced, by life, to unknowingly start searching for answers. That is what I felt compelled to do since my life became a hardship after an incident that shook me emotionally.

My baby sister Nicky was my constant companion for a short time. All three of us, me, my older sister and my brother, had the responsibility to take care of her at times. As a man, our brother helped when he felt like it, but did not have to do so. This was very common back then.

We played and sang. Mom spent so much time teaching us how to take care of baby Nicky; showing us what to do when she would be too busy to care of "Baby" that it now became second nature. She showed us how to kiss her hands, her cheeks and be gentle with her as well as feeding her from the bottle.

But, Nicky always seemed to be crying about something.

After returning from the doctor, Nicky received a clear bill of health. We thought she was colicky, but the family physician assured us that there was nothing wrong.

One night while our parents had friends over, Nicky began crying and would not stop.

"Baby why are you crying?"

She continued to wail and wail. Nicky and I had communicated many times before. Call it perception, mental images, or telepathy; I could understand her. She was crying with all her might that evening as I continued: "Nicky, why are you crying."

Suddenly a really sharp pain wrapped itself around my stomach and then pierced me like a knife. I cannot explain it specifically, but it was so painful! I doubled over and for some unknown reason, I wondered if I was feeling her pain. Was she projecting it onto me so I could understand how she felt? Somehow, I knew, THAT, was how she was feeling. And in a voiceless voice, she communicated her distress to me.

I left her side and ran to the living room to tell my parents what I believed Nicky had just told me telepathically. "Baby has pain in her stomach. We gotta go to the doctor now!" In front of the guests my mom looked at me dumbfounded.

"What are you talking about little girl? Go play with your sister!" She snapped at me.

"But mommy Nicky has bad pain, here, in her tummy (stomach) here mom…" Trying to touch and show everyone where I myself had felt the pain.

"The doctor says she is fine. Go play, shake her rattle, and she will stop crying. "

"No mommy, no! Nicky is sick. "

I went back to Nicky disappointed and unable to speak for her. I told her "Nicky I told mom but she does not believe me. She won't listen baby." We were communicating soul to soul.

Once again I heard the same distinct voiceless voice from inside of me, saying, "That's fine, Nicky is leaving soon anyway!" This is how we had always communicated with each other. I replied: "Baby why you want to leave us? Why Nicky?" I then knew the answer to my question. Nicky had some sort of blockage in her stomach and she would suffer for the rest of her life. She kept crying and there was nothing I can do to console her. As I put my small hand between the bars of her crib to touch her again, mom showed up. "You are not shaking the rattle, are you?" "My hands are hurting." I replied.

I continued, "Nicky is going to leave us Mommy." "She did not come to stay a long-time, she says"

I started to cry for many reasons, unable to process my emotions at the tender age of 4. I was experiencing sadness about Nicky's suffering. I was born an empath. I could feel her pain. I just had no words to describe it to others. Besides, she let me know that she was leaving. I naturally trusted that piece of information but did not ask her where she was going. Inside this higher space where Nicky and I communicated, our mom could not enter nor comprehend the possibilities existing from which people can interact through awareness or inner knowingness. Having no clue about her daughters' reality,

102

there is no way our mother could believe the message I had been trying to convey!

I do not know what happened next because it all happened so quickly. Nicky stopped crying as Mom comforted her. My mother screamed and Dad rushed into the room, grabbed her to rush outside, heading to the hospital. Mom was crying hysterically and grandma had her arms around mommy saying, "She is not breathing normally!"

The next morning my brother and I were taken to our aunt's house never knowing what took place. A week later, early on a Sunday, our uncle picked us up.

The whole family was dressed in their Sunday best, waiting for us. We then drove to Mass. Mom and Dad sat in the front with Dad driving. The three of us kids were in the backseat without Nicky's chair. As we passed by the cemetery located right beside the church, my older sister reached out to hold my hand and took it upon herself to tell me what exactly happened while my brother and I were away from home.

"This is where Nicky is now! She is not at home." She whispered in my ear, pointing at the cemetery. It made no sense to me. I asked: "Here! Why?"

My sister continued the story as the car rolled along the sun beaten mountainsides of the island of Haiti.

"Dad put Baby Nicky on a coffin bed. He covered her and left her inside a little house" (referring to our family mausoleum).

"Mom cried but our father took me and Mom in the car and we all went home without the baby."

"Dad leaves the baby all by herself?"

"Uh Huh… I was there. I saw him do that!"

"Why? Was Nicky crying too much?"

I did not know anything about burial or death. I was confused thinking it was just a harsh punishment and that she would be home soon when someone went back to pick her up.

"No, Grandma says she is dead."

"Who is there to play with her?"

"She cannot play. Baby is dead."

I could not understand death at such a young age. I simply did not feel good that my father put her in that coffin bed as my sister called it, and left her alone inside a cemetery where there was nobody for her to play with, or feed her the bottle.

"What did she do to make Dad angry at her?"

"I don't know. I told you she died. You don't get it" My older sister was impatient at this point. She understood more than the rest of us. Clearly she was tired of my lack of understanding.

I held my father responsible for the baby's death. I took it as cruelty inflicted by our father upon our little sister! That is all I could understand. My heart felt heavy and tight. That is the day I cried. Was it really for Nicky that I cried, or was it over my own fear of death?

My mind totally ignored the last conversation I had with Nicky the night before she passed away. Instantly, I become petrified of my father for his actions, resenting even his presence. I thought that he might put me in a coffin to leave me in the cemetery if I was not a good girl.

I did not dare ask my older sister any more questions, though many swirled around in my head.

Now it was only the two of us, me and my brother in the house when our sister goes to school. I was still expecting Nicky to be back…

Every Sunday mom used to stop to buy us patties on the way home from mass. (Meat or vegetables wrapped in a light French pastry dough is a traditional Haitian patty.) But today we went straight home. Mom did not give us a thing! I continued begging and pleading for the baby's return. That must have added to our family's grief. No one went for her and no one knew how to explain the process of death to me either.

Two weeks later, when going to Mass again I asked, "When will we pick up Nicky?"

No one answered. Then my sister broke the silence "Don't say that! You are making Mommy cry."

Later, that same day, Mom called me over. I usually went to her skipping, but this time was different. I approached with caution. From the tone of my mother's voice I knew that I was not about to be praised.

"Yes mommy!"

Mother proceeds with a sermon. "Listen to me! From now on, I do not want you to predict anything for anybody in the family. You are not to say that 'bad things' will happen to people. You hear me? You seem to have a bad mouth. You can actually make things happen for real when you say them out loud. You must stop talking! Do you get it?"

Half listening, I answered, "I did not say bad words mommy. See grandma is here! See?" I pointed to my grandmother sitting in the shade, hoping she would vouch for me.

Still not seizing the meaning of this message my mother was trying to convey, I remained in front of her, unable to connect to what she was telling me. My mother's eyes were filled with tears as she started addressing the 4-year old me. I can never forget the pain in her eyes as she searched for the right words, attempting to explain that Nicky would never be coming home again because she lived in Heaven now.

To me Nicky is in a small house by the cemetery.

"You say that Nicky would die, right? Remember that?" Mom's tears were streaming down her cheeks.

"Tell me why you said she would die! You did not want to play with her, right? Is that why?"

I was feeling cornered, without the proper vocabulary to explain or to defend myself. In a desperate attempt to shift the blame, I brought up my father as the guilty party, the one who left Nicky alone. "No mom, it's not me! It's Dad who did that mommy, not me!" I began to cry, thinking that I caused my little sister to die, whatever death is.

"Dad did what? Remember you said to me she is going to die? Why did you wish that on your sister?" I then associate that night with the Baby's departure.

"Mom, baby Nicky talked to me. She spoke in my head! She told me she was leaving!"

I was telling the truth. Why was mom so upset with me? She questioned me, without realizing that to me, Nicky saying that she is leaving did not mean that she was dying to be buried later and never to come back home; It wasn't a concept I had in mind, or even understood.

Blurting out what actually occurred that late evening, I explained it in the best way I could that Nicky and I had a telepathic connection, by saying she "spoke in my head." But this concept was totally foreign to my mother, and definitely outside the norm of her strict religious upbringing.

Most of these principles were not a secret to Napoleon Hill who had already written his book "Think and Grow Rich" in 1937, in which specialized knowledge and secret communication with an invisible council of advisors was discussed and clearly explained. Sadly, my mother was not part of the few in life who were privileged enough to discover the great secrets of success in order to use her mental capacities, advance in life and grow rich.

Principles of quantum physics or quantum mechanics were considered to be mumbo jumbo by the average mind; not mainstream knowledge as it is slowly becoming now.

My innate abilities appear strange or unbelievable except for those who experienced them as their reality as I have.

I promised my mom "When Baby comes back home and cries, I will play with her and shake her rattle."

"You must stop saying that. I will not go get her from the grave. It's impossible for me to do that!"

"Send grandma, Mom."

"Baby will not come back here! You will not see her ever again until you die too and go to Heaven. You did not want to play with Nicky, remember that?"

That was the last time I mentioned death. Too scary for a four-year old!

"No, I don't want to die too!"

She scoffs at me again: "I'm going to punish you for making things up!" Being so firm added to the disagreement brought a sense of shame and guilt to my conscious self for the first time. Something constricted in my world, and I felt smaller.

We are trained to say "yes" when being reprimanded by our parents and not to talk back. Not knowing how to act or react at this point, I remained silent. As she continued to talk, although I wanted to keep arguing, to explain myself more, I stop as my father enters the room and confronts me. I had been petrified by his actions and now quite confused by my mother.

"Did I hear you talking back to your mom? I am so disappointed in you with your fertile imagination! Be quiet and listen!"

In our family, we must tell the truth, no lying! And no exceptions! So I told the truth, yet my parents' reactions forced me to deny the reality of an inner interaction between us (me and Nicky). They asked me to accept that I made things up. Afraid of punishment, I mumbled yes and kept my head down. Tears streaming down my face.

Suddenly a forceful energy blocked my voice. I see my mother's mouth moving, but I no longer hear one single world. There is no more interaction between her world and mine.

I feel being bad for making mom cry. I feel responsible for whatever happened to Baby Nicky that evening, thinking her death is somehow my fault.

For the very first time negative feelings of remorse, shame, and blame enter my heart. Discomfort, distortion and confinement took over my inner peace. I was sent to stand behind a door as my punishment. I had to agree with my parents, denying my own truth to make them right, to make them happy inside their world. I must repeat, "I will not make things up any more, I will not lie again." I had to. There was no choice at that moment.

I felt alone knowing that my mom and dad did not understand me. I wanted to regain their love. So, I tried to comfort them by being a good girl; playing a role in life to please others. But it was a very detrimental way of going through life. I was not authentic.

The innocent little girl full of joy that I once was, the bubbly daughter, had stopped talking. It was impossible to reconcile being authentic, and at the same time, meet my parent's expectations. At home I could not be me. I could not stand up for myself. I resented the way I felt after that incident. It becomes such a habit of denying my personal experiences that I doubted and questioned if really those telepathic communications actually took place. A part of me knows for sure that they did occur, but my parent's conviction that I had lied infiltrates my belief in me.

As doubt enters my world, it weakens these innate abilities I was born with.

As a child all was possible. I could see energy in or around things; I could see what is called The Matrix, hear people's thought forms, and communicate from a distance with just my mind. Yes, before my sister's death, anything and everything was possible to me.

Afterwards, I withdrew, doubting everything I believed in or experienced.

From that moment on, our house was rearranged with fewer and fewer reminders of Nicky's presence. With time nobody mentions her at all. Life keeps evolving and I no longer ask for her to return. The family's memory of little Nicky slowly fades away. But for me, fear, uncertainty and death itself would remain a mystery for many years to come.

That incident changed me. With a flame burning slowly within my heart, I wanted to change my life at many levels to know joy and freedom again. I was already seeing beauty in all life, yet realizing that there must be a Master Creator to arrange things so harmoniously despite all the cacophony and the randomnity.

I came to this realization that something exists which creates such a harmonious rhythm and beauty around life, that I desire to discover it, know it and experience it. Whether this Master Creator is being represented or is being manifested by some great-expanded energy, God, a teacher, a Higher Power, an ocean or unconditioned loving feelings, I was determined to find it throughout life.

In starting this chapter for "Journeys to Success" book, I found myself taking a good look back to view the gap between then and now. Aware of where I stand right in this moment to share my experiences or observations, helps me to determine how I'd applied the many laws and principles of life so far, for my personal success. I refer to Success as being more than just money. We are talking about the sum total of different aspects of this life that I'm now leading, the life that I have created.

Consciously or unconsciously, we are the creators of our own reality.

Therefore, whatever I'd achieved in this lifetime, I always remember to give thanks to all those that entered my life at one point or another to teach me and to cause my view to be heightened or enlarged. Through lessons coming from nature, animals, or other human beings, life taught me constantly throughout the years. We meet the people on our way like our spouses, our birth family, sibling or friends who make everything much easier or much more difficult for us.

They are all teachers that helped us reshape, recognize true love, find wisdom, and reach freedom from a nonjudgmental state of being. From you all wonderful souls out there, it has been imperative for me to first learn

110

discernment and graciousness. For, these two characteristics became key elements of survival. After immigrating to the US, too obedient and too trustworthy, I was just like the same 4-year old girl, except I no longer believed in Santa Claus. Oh, have I learned and grown!

Lots of you provided support that filled me with love, appreciation, strength and contentment, which helped establish my platform in life today. From the heightened awareness where I am positioned to view this moment and to enjoy life to the fullest, I am still growing, still learning, I could not have achieved it without your contributions, whether loving or even brutally painful towards me. I learn from all life.

Regardless, what matters now is for me to simply BE, know and connect with the real self in life. Call it God, your Higher Power, Great Architect, I AM Presence, Ocean of Love and Grace etc. for me, IT has always been guiding my every step, decision making, loving me, providing, protecting, supporting and flowing through me, expanding through me.

When too young to name IT, I could only feel IT bringing me comfort whenever I needed solace...especially after Nicky's death. Unbeknownst to me at the tender age of four, I became a seeker.

My Definite Purpose Draws Me To New York City

As an adolescent, I had been telling everybody that someday I would live in the United States of America. No one paid attention to me because immigrating in a foreign country involves more than a visa. I had no one close enough living in the USA that would agree to fill out legal papers on my behalf. So my mom always reminded me of that, "You are going nowhere!"

"Oh, yes, Mom I will go! You watch and see!"

While girls my age are mostly concerned with falling in love or enjoying life, I wanted to find a way to change or upgrade my personal life. The greatest desire in my heart was to leave. Meaning I will leave behind everyone that I love, all I'm accustomed to, for the uncertainty of a foreign country. Not that weird however, if you can understand the infrastructure of some foreign countries.

Though I did not speak English, did not understand the culture, and had no specific skills to find employment in the US of America, I still knew immigrating was the right thing to do. Intense determination to change my life overshadowed everything else. One morning, I took my passport, headed to the consulate and returned home with a ticket to come back later for my stamped passport, my freedom to enter the US legally.

"No one around me could imagine this to be possible in their wildest dreams!" Mom proclaimed while I was singing and dancing saying. "I am going to the US, going to the US!"

That was the last month I spent at my parents' house before coming to the United States. Suddenly the thought of leaving became a nightmare. Was it the right thing to do? It was too much for me to bear. Being torn apart would be an understatement. My father helped the best he could by making connections to assure that I will be safe. He helped financially. That is when I realized how much their children meant to my parents.

They made mistakes like any human beings because as humans, we do not know what we don't know. Nevertheless they truly loved us wholeheartedly.

An early morning, my father offered to drive me to the airport later. Dad was very concerned as I declined. I had to do this alone! I grabbed my suitcase and kissed mom good-bye! My siblings left for work and did not even call home to talk to me.

The sadness around me was almost the same as the day Nicky passed away.

My mother was the strongest member of our family. She stayed at home until I headed to the airport. She crumbled at the last minute. I went outside, raised my hands to call a taxi and never turned back. If I had looked in my mother's eyes, I probably would not have had the courage to pursue my journey. I left with the idea of having an opportunity to create new avenues and make life better for all of us.

This move to the United States is a new chapter in my life's adventures.

As soon as I left the comfort of my parents' niche, that's when my real odyssey began! Coming to NYC is when I am forced to really search for answers.

I soon concluded that life set me up from the start in order to upgrade my state of awareness and put me onto the true path of conscious awakening. My entire life was and is a journey of self-discovery!

Forced to learn fast, not having the luxury for relaxation in the hustle and bustle of a big city, I developed the skills to obtain the knowledge I seek at lightning speed. I read a lot and learn a lot that's for sure.

Specialized knowledge, natural abilities, telepathic communication and seeing the quantum field with eyes opened or closed were not common knowledge among the average person. Yet they were innate abilities for me as I established a sense of what was happening within, as well as around myself.

Intangible and unseen phenomena were not part of the everyday conversation at our family dinner table as I was growing up. However, they have always been a part of everyday life for many, who were just like me.

While living in the US, I heard about pioneers like Emile Coue, the French psychotherapist who taught auto suggestion; Nikola Tesla and Thomas Edison, who discovered how to harness electricity and make usage of it worldwide. I learned about Dr. Emoto who published studies on quantum physics and quantum mechanics, which explained how thoughts could affect matter. A French chemist named Pasteur is the first to discover that germs cause disease. Nowadays, no one seems to ignore the fact that the atom is no longer known as the smallest particles there is; quarks and photons are.

All of these references are part of what cannot be seen with our naked eyes, aren't they?

Even with so many scientific proofs, many principles are still called mumbo jumbo by lots of educated minds that refuse to reconsider that their own thoughts actually create their reality. No matter what, the possibility that something cannot be a part of our experiences will reveal to the "believer" that it cannot; without their awareness that it is their thinking that keeps the solutions at bay.

Our beliefs can place limitations on our life, or expand it.

Yes, as a child, I did communicate beyond the realms of spoken words. It is not that I am superior, special or different and have something that others do not. Each and every one of us carries this God seed or master cell within us. There are the aspects of us that we ignore or avoid talking about as we rush off to work.

Any ability such as mindfulness, soul awareness, wholeness, or living in the Divine Presence can be developed. First the awareness or acceptance of these skills is required. We can have dominion over matter, energy, space and time. Again, this is our birthright!

Apparently I was not meant to grow up totally unconscious. My life has a purpose. Part of me knew it from the start! Children do not come to earth as dummies.

Summer of 2016, today in New York City, I am reading "Think And Grow Rich" by Napoleon Hill. I feel like Dorothy in the Wizard of Oz, having to leave a dusty gray world of painful lessons in life, and of disillusion to now partake of a greater and illuminated state of consciousness. After discovering such a bright and expansive world in which love, inner joy and contentment are the norm, I regain my confidence.

In this unified field within our heart, we remain connected to our Divine Source at each moment. We are IT. No judgments. It is an expansive space where we become both, a conscious creator and creation itself. All the while completely experiencing our own reality in this unifying consciousness where ALL IS ONE, ALL is celebrated.

This awareness started from childhood. It started with Nicky's death. I was no different than any other child except that life had begun to shake me and wake me up from an early stage. From that day on, I was watchful, vigilant, and question everyone that comes my way and everything in front of me. This only started my quest for truth in order for me to aim for the highest there is. It kept me awake by paying attention to that, which leads to oneness, freedom, power and divine wisdom known as the qualities of the Divine.

I stand in life today to realize how I applied the many laws or principles for my own success. Again, I refer to more than just money when mentioning success. It is more than the financial aspect of life. It is about the sum total of different aspects of our life such as spirituality, love, relationships, career, personal enjoyment, and achieving my life purpose.

I not only discover myself, but I love myself wholeheartedly, without judgment, simply total acceptance of self and others, total responsibility for what is in my field of awareness, freedom, love and wisdom. Within my heart and soul, I know the Divine is always present.

I must admit it took me way more than 36 hours for such a realization, unlike young Gunsaulus in the case of the million-dollar manifestation story told by Napoleon Hill. It actually took me over 20 years for shifts to start occurring, overthrowing habits, dropping subconscious beliefs, taking responsibility for my own life and creations, while realizing the I AM presence that we are.

In Napoleon Hill's story, Gunsaulus needed a million dollars to put a new method of education into place. In 36 hours, he was able to manifest the money by successfully using the success principles that Hill wrote about. No matter how long it takes, when we learn to discover ourselves by working with the principles of life, we are on the road to mastership.

In my case, recognizing where I am and where I wanted to be, seeking Specialized Knowledge was required with each step to establish my heartfelt desires. I learned how to let my heart and mind be connected in order to flow harmoniously with the rhythm of life as I expand more and more. Often times, relying on groups or institutions that promise but do not deliver, often watching communities bringing each other down to a place of judgment. Learning to take action becomes imperative for us to thrive on our own journey to success! Indeed, learning to trust one-self becomes a must on this path.

If we realize that we can only be restrained by our own limitation we allow ourselves to be bold and adventuresome as we simply keep moving forward and letting go of fear!
The truth is:

"The only limitation is that which one sets up in one's own mind."

**Let us fully live each and every moment in loving trust, like
Godly Beings!**

BIO

Norma Edmond became a Hospice Care Nurse a few years ago, after being a geriatric then a pediatric nurse, providing care for newborns, infants and toddlers for over 25 years. Her compassionate nature is so well known, patients and their families often request her by name.

Prior to nursing, she dwelled within the world of finance as a Certified Financial Advisor for one of New York's largest insurance companies and a technologist, studying computer programming in college. From sales to entrepreneurship, Norma has built multiple businesses from the ground up through the years.

Today, she enjoys life as a poet, writer and simultaneous translator nationally for live events from English/French/English. She continues on her journey of self-development, empowering not only herself, but others.

She now lives in NYC with her husband Brad. On weekends, she visits her mom, dad and sister in Long Island, NY. She helped her parents make the move to the United States over 25 years ago.

She can be reached at norma@liquidleadership.com

SUCCESS: THE SOCRATIC HOPE IN OUR LIVES

By: J. Ibeh Agbanyim

In a world where there is no sky, what would stop one from achieving their highest potential? This is a challenging question because past experiences and memories could establish the sky as a limit for people reaching for their potential.

Growing up as a child, it was obvious that there were limitations and boundaries that existed in human minds. But, in the midst of those limitations and boundaries, society, family members, and friends placed on us, either by default, or the ones we placed on ourselves, achieving our greatest potential is still attainable.

From a personal perspective, in order to challenge my internal prison walls and rise above my obstacles, it takes Napoleon Hill's principles of:

- Definite of purpose

- Self-discipline

- Accurate thinking

- Teamwork

For the next few pages, we are going to take mental flights, reading how applying Napoleon Hill's principles of Success helped me to achieve my goals in the areas of job longevity, education, and book publishing and are helping me to understand my purpose in life, and extending lessons learned along the way to impacting others. This chapter was written to share the importance of goal-setting and taking action to achieve those goals.

I strategically focus this chapter around three areas in my life that have proven to be stable and measurable, using Napoleon Hill's principles of success as a propellant to my success in these areas. The measurable accomplishments discussed in this text are; job longevity, education, and book publishing. This will serve as a model that readers can relate to their own lives.

Definite of Purpose

Job Longevity

According to Napoleon Hill's definiteness of purpose principle, without a definite purpose it is difficult to achieve significant and measurable goals in life. In other words, for one to achieve a goal there is a need for a clear purpose. Over two decades ago I found Napoleon Hill's principle of definite purpose relevant in my career search. Prior to discovering Hill's principles of success, I was bouncing from one job to another thinking that somehow I could find myself a well paying job. But the danger about my untested assumption was that, I had no definite purpose, so it was difficult to articulate what I wanted in life. The moment that I decided to find a job that paid well and had benefits, and that allowed me the flexibility to pursue other goals, securing a job that had longevity became a priority, because I made a conscious decision to make the strategic shift. I am fortunate to say that since 1997 I have retained a job at a logistics company for nineteen years. My decision to stay at one company for this many years was motivated by studying the work of Napoleon Hill. The benefit of having a definite purpose is that it gives me a clear picture of my life. Second, it creates stability. Because of my ability to work at a company for this many years, I was able to plan my next project in life without worrying about how to make ends meet.

As a result of nineteen years of job security, I was able to purchase a home at an early stage in my career. The idea of owning a piece of real estate was a confirmation that a definite purpose organizes and positions a person for success. From a psychological standpoint, a definite purpose gives me mental stability and emotional stability. Mental stability in a sense that I had less worry about how to meet physiological needs such as food, shelter, clothes and so forth. From an emotional stability standpoint, my stress life was healthy and stable. Invariably, my life was stable as a result of defining my objectives and pursuing them strategically, especially focusing on how to secure job longevity. In this context, a definite purpose had a measurable outcome because I was able to meet physiological goals, job longevity, purchase a home, and maintain mental and emotional stability.

A Definite purpose also has a spillover effect. This means that, when there is a definite purpose, it is easier to set long-term goals. For example, going back to school was promising as a result of a definite purpose. From a humanitarian perspective, I was able to sponsor family members and anybody who showed an interest in education and a degree. It was much easier to help others once I had job security. It was even more pronounced when focusing on defined tasks that are practical and simplified. Because there was a clear goal, self-discipline was required to maintain focus, particularly in my academic pursuits. I see myself as lifetime student, therefore there is never a dull moment when it comes to reading books and learning from all fields of endeavors.

Self-Discipline

Education

If education is the key to success, what is the door? It is a common saying that "education is the key to success." but have we ever wondered what the door that one is trying to open is? Napoleon Hill's principles of success helped me to answer the question. The door that education is trying to open is ME—My Mind. By reading Think and Grow Rich, it was clear to me that my mind is the most powerful door to unlock. The moment my mind is unlocked, there is no limit to what possibilities are ahead.

It is clear to me that Napoleon Hill's principles of success serve as building blocks to becoming a well-rounded person. A Definite purpose is a mental road map for human development. In my experience, without a definite purpose, it was difficult to be disciplined in pursuing my goals. For example, I was able to pursue my education because my basic needs were met through applying a definite purpose in securing job longevity. Acquiring my first degree was challenging due to time conflicts with my work but, because I already had a clear goal on why I should pursue my education, I was able to negotiate my social life so that I could. Accommodating study time meant collaborating with my company to ensure that my goal aligned with company goals. It was challenging for management to accommodate my school schedule but, because I involved management, it made the experience inclusive and achievable. Self-discipline was also at the center of my academic pursuits.

Self-discipline is clearly required for achieving goals. Napoleon Hill's principle of self-discipline supports the idea that mastery of thought is critical. Self-discipline requires a marriage between what I think and how I feel. These two constructs must work in balance for a person to live a full life. Without balancing my emotions and thoughts, completing my degree program would have been impossible because my emotions were fluctuating based on circumstances either at work, at home, or even while staying alone. On the other hand, I also wanted to align with my unstable emotions to quit school and only focus on my 9-6-work schedule. Because of my commitment to a definite purpose, accomplishing my academic objectives became a necessity. In 2005, the National Science Foundation said that an average brain processes about 12,000 to 60,000 thoughts daily and 80 percent of those thoughts are negative. Ninety-five percent of those negative thoughts are repetitive thoughts. Based on this statistical evidence, it was critical to discipline my thoughts so that I could complete my academic program.

Discussing education from a formal standpoint requires structure and a system in place. This means setting aside study time, and time to attend courses online, in person or through a blended program. On the other hand, an informal approach to education requires more attention to wisdom from people who have acquired knowledge from experiences in their areas of pursuits. For example, parents, mentors, pastors, guardians, and so forth are some of the examples of people who are extending informal education into our lives. To be able to combine these two approaches to learning I must be disciplined in my thoughts and emotions. Napoleon Hill's principles of success clearly have influenced how I have worked in the same company for a long period of time, and was able to complete my undergrad and graduate degrees as well. This is evidence that having a definite purpose, applying self-discipline and translating thoughts into actions definitely helps achieve measurable goals.

In 2012, I decided to dive into publishing my first book, The Power of Engagement. The book chronicled how goal setting and engagement can help people balance work and life in a busy world. Goal setting and engagement work hand in hand because, without having a definite purpose, it will be difficult to mentally and physically engage in whatever task one sets out to accomplish. Clear thinking is critical in organizing thoughts and resources, and translating thoughts into measurable goals. It was on this quest of accurate thinking, as written about by Napoleon Hill, that I associated myself with bestselling authors who helped me achieve my goal of publishing books.

Accurate Thinking and Teamwork

Book Publishing

Publishing my first book was inspired by knowledge gained from reading Napoleon Hill's Think and Grow Rich, along with other self-motivational authors such as Dr. Norman Vincent Peale and other authors of similar caliber. Napoleon Hill's quote: "All you need is one sound idea to succeed," was quoted in my first book, The Power of Engagement, suggesting that, if we can guard our thoughts and ideas, we can translate such thoughts into success. It is obvious that a definite purpose is a necessary ingredient of life. Dr. Hill's principles of success help me to understand the importance of focusing on one task at a time until that task is completed. Publishing my first book has opened other doors and has motivated me to publish two other books. I am working on a fourth book that will be ready for publication in the summer of 2016.

Since the publication of my first book in 2012, I have helped five other authors publish their books, and many others are in the process of completing their manuscripts for publication. It is obvious that success is infectious. This paradigm shift confirms Napoleon Hill's principle of Teamwork. His principle of Teamwork suggested that success is inevitable where there is free spirit and collaboration with people. I find this to be true because, from my experience, many people have been influenced as a result of me staying focused, controlling my thoughts, and working with others to achieve their potential. By staying focused and self-disciplined, my work has helped me connect with many successful authors and entrepreneurs. Successful authors' and entrepreneurs' contributions with my work placed my recent book, The Five Principles of Collaboration into multiple Amazon Bestselling book categories. Knowledge gained from Napoleon Hill's work has definitely positioned me to influence young adults, business leaders, and employees alike.

Napoleon Hill's accurate thinking principle has helped me think critically in pursing my goals. In one instance, accurate thinking positioned me to look at a situation objectively and logically before making decisions. I obtained my first degree through the traditional way of education. I was attending classes four hours once a week, writing numerous school papers, and endless PowerPoint Slides presentations, while holding a 50+ hour per week work schedule. Due to the tediousness of my work schedule, it took me seven years to complete a four-year degree program. Having experienced a hectic schedule in completing my first degree, I was not willing to resign from my many years working at the logistics company to pursue my education; I decided to pursue my graduate degree through a traditional university in Phoenix, Arizona that also runs a virtual program. The virtual program approach, with a physical campus, gave me the flexibility to attend campus workshops and seminars, use the campus library, access to professors, and also to experience campus life on weekends. I was able to structure my schoolwork according to online modalities, which gave me time on weekends to complete course assignments and write research papers. Accurate thinking and a definite purpose were critical components that helped me to manage between 25 hours/week of course work and a 50+-hour work schedule. It was clear in my mind that I wanted to achieve my goals of keeping my long-term job security, pursue my education, and publish books. Because of having a definite purpose, self-discipline, accurate thinking, and teamwork, I was able to organize like-minded people who share the same interests in education, writing, and job security. It made sense to me that a definite purpose, self-discipline, and accurate thinking had helped me to achieve my goals up until this point. Teamwork is a critical component that brings humanity into practice and unison. I do recognize the importance of healthy human relationships and altruism. They are the cornerstones for all mankind to live in a world where there is no sky.

Ongoing Lessons from Napoleon Hill's 17 Principles of Success

Based on my experience with Napoleon Hill's 17 Principles of Success, I believe there are principles that transform lives across age, gender, nationality, religion, and so forth. The Principles also emphasize the importance of giving. Giving is one practice that has altruistic values and spiritual fulfillment. I embrace Napoleon Hill's 17 principles of success because they are practical and measurable. I view the principles as a road map to achieving my potential. In the areas of Job Longevity, Education, and

Book Publishing, the principles have proven to be time tested and consistent in my journey. The principles are ongoing and dynamic.

One of the reasons for pursuing a PhD in psychology is rooted from applying Napoleon Hill's principles in my journey. I noticed that Hill's principles indiscriminately improve personal growth and relationships in every spectrum of life. Hill's principles touch every core of human existence, particularly in the area of self-efficacy (knowing thyself). When I decided to pursue a PhD, it was clear to me that in the process of writing my dissertation I also rediscovered myself through reading case studies, evidenced-based research, experiments, and asking categorical and critical research questions. For doctoral candidates to complete their degree program there has to be a definite purpose around why students want to pursue such degrees. A Doctoral dissertation program requires students to write a Purpose Statement, Problem Statement, and Research Questions. This is an indication of a journey that has a clear goal, accurate thinking, self-discipline, teamwork, and other principles shared by Napoleon Hill. It is evident that staying on course with Napoleon Hill's principles in the context of completing a doctoral degree directs and prepares students for success. Second, teamwork is one principle that is inevitable in completing a doctoral program. A team of dissertation committee members including a dissertation supervisor, content expert, methodologist, and Institute of Review Board come together to ensure that quality and successful work is achieved. Third, a successful completion of a doctoral program benefits the graduate and humanity, because the wealth of knowledge gained from the dissertation journey are expressed and demonstrated through a graduate's area of expertise. For example, completing my doctoral degree in organizational psychology helps me answer workplace related issues that arise in organizations including employee disengagement, job dissatisfaction, increasing employee morale, employee turnover, selection process, motivation, and a whole host of other dire challenges organizations face on a daily basis. Applying Hill's fundamental principles of definite purpose, self-discipline, accurate thinking, and teamwork prepares me to reach for higher goals and impact individuals in a local and global context. Hill's principles of success challenge me on a daily basis to be self-aware, focused, collaborate, and altruistic. There is no limit to what the human mind can do when put into work.

BIO

J. Ibeh Agbanyim is a Harvard trained leadership coaching strategist, Amazon bestselling author, public speaker, and organizational psychology consultant. He is the president of Focused Vision Consulting, LLC; a management consulting firm. He works with organizations and individuals on how to live a life of impact by applying the Five Principles of Collaboration. Nineteen years of working in logistics helps Ibeh understand the importance of effective teamwork and how collaboration contributes to organizational and individual well-being.

Ibeh has presented his work to various organizations, institutions, and individuals on how to translate thoughts into actions, focusing on positive psychology and desired thinking. He has presented at the American Society for Quality, Orlando, FL; George Washington University, Washington, DC; University of Ibadan, Nigeria, collaborated with International Conference for Psychological Science in Amsterdam, The Netherlands, and presented at University of Ghana, 2016 School of Sciences International Conference on the topic, Fear: The Invisible Determinant. He also presented his work at Arizona State University Project Humanities, facilitated by Dr. Neal Lester, Director of ASU project Humanities.

He recently shared the stage with the Mayor of Tempe, Arizona, Mark Mitchell, and former congressman Harry Mitchell during the Don Carlos Humanitarian Awards event at Tempe Community Council, Tempe, Arizona. He was an invited guest at the Arizona State University's W. P. Carey School of Business 2015 Spirit of Enterprise Awards, and the Napoleon Hill Stickability conference in Toronto, Canada. Ibeh is a reviewer for the Association for Psychological Science Student Caucus, and scholarly contributor as a peer reviewer in Journal of Instructional Research at Grand Canyon University. Ibeh is the author of three books, The Power of Engagement, Fear, and an Amazon Bestselling book, The Five Principles of Collaboration. He is working on his fourth book due out this summer.

Ibeh earned his master's degree in industrial-organizational psychology and is pursuing his PhD in the same subject. When he is not busy with work, dissertations, and speaking engagements, he loves to hike, spends time with friends and family, and engages in music therapy for relaxation.

He can be reached at powerofengagement@att.net, www.fvgrowth.com, https://www.linkedin.com/in/j-ibeh-agbanyim-ms-i-o-8513322b

THE ART OF PERSISTENCE
By: Tony Fevola

Sometimes the most difficult thing to do is to start, though this is certainly not the end of my story. My name is Tony Fevola. I am a person who is genuinely one of the hardest working and generously collaborative people on this planet. This is my belief. Whether true or untrue, I have always realized that the powerful words "I AM," are what I set to my mind and create. Recognizing and respecting my purpose in life is as important, if not more important, than all of the goals and accomplishments I have had along the way. Having my story shared in this collection is one way to have my long and varied experiences serve as a model for those who may read it.

As an immigrant son of parents coming from Southern Italy in 1969, my start in America was already two steps behind from the very beginning. America has been founded on the backs of immigrants, and I, as an immigrant child, have joined the rather elite ranks of others who have arrived in America before me. This country has welcomed me but has also had its many obstacles which I sometimes still work hard to overcome. Opening businesses, developing clientele and networking connections comes easily to me in that I am an affable man of my word, but it has presented me challenges along the way, no one is here to help, it is every man for himself. Through many attempts, both successful and not so successful, I have learned to become self-reliant and persistent in pursuing what I want. While the traditional paradigm is that hard work automatically leads to success, I learned when I was young, that all I needed to do was to imagine what I wanted and then it would be easier to work towards manifesting it.

Although my parents are the ones who made the difficult decision to come here to seek the American Dream, I am the person who was actually able to define it for myself and for them. They came here simply because other family members had told them that life would be better on this side of the Atlantic. I think that they may actually have been told that the streets were paved with gold! AI, as a child had no choice as to where I would be raised, and I made the decision that my dream, American or Italian, would be one I chose to follow and create throughout my life. I knew intrinsically that I am the only one who can make my vision into a reality. I envision and am able to create, seemingly out of the ether. These words in this book being an example of one of the many things I have sought to achieve and now you're reading them!

Very few people would voluntarily leave a home overlooking the Mediterranean to life in a family shared overcrowded apartment in Brooklyn, interacting in a language alien to the ears and NOT see their mother and father daily. I, along with my older siblings, was brought here and had to learn to get along in this new world. With the cards seemingly stacked against me I just knew I would make it. One thing I am is PERSISTENT! Once I make up my mind to do or achieve something, once I have seen it in my mind's eye, I will move heaven and earth to make it happen. This new language, English, became mine and I use it to full advantage in all my interactions. I read and write daily, fine-tuning my ideas and the way that I express myself. I have made a point of reading the works of Shakespeare, American writers and also classic self- help and psychological pieces by authors like Stephen Covey, Brian Tracy, and Jim Rohn. Their down to earth, pragmatic assessments blended and synthesized perfectly with the more esoteric, yet meaningful pieces of fiction I have devoured over the years. I have grown to see that the message in all of these works is present everywhere, it just means opening my heart or mind to it.

Far from being the typical American Dream family, early on we moved into New Jersey so my father could start a business. This, unfortunately for us, meant living separately with different relatives until my parents could reunite us into a single home. Most children, at least in America, and in all the storybooks that I had read, did not have to endure this kind of separation when young. I realize that home is where the heart is but the size of our new home was small, unfamiliar and not at all what I had long envisioned or had been promised. When we were separated, I lived with an aunt, uncle and cousin. I knew that even though it wasn't my home, it was a home. I was more than determined to make certain that my own family would have one. I saw what it looked like, knew what it felt like and all I had to do was share my vision with my parents and family. I would draw picture after picture of the house that I dreamed of. As I fell asleep at night I would close my eyes and see it as I drifted off to sleep, praying my intent. I, being more American already through schools and television, saw things through the possibilities of what could be, what must be, and my tenacity of spirit and doggedness with my parents ultimately got them to look for, find and purchase a home! This is one of the earliest instances of my identifying a struggle or challenge of living as we did, knowing that life could and must be different! I was able to see it and share my vision with my family. I still work hard at identifying, describing and working through challenges as they invariably face us all.

American life brought other challenges. Being able to fit into school and achieve, at least the way it looked like on television or in my mind was a constant goal. I would work hard at my schoolwork and face insurmountable frustrations when my parents who were not sophisticated in English would not encourage or help me in a productive way. They did not know how to do it; they were raising my siblings and me as though we still lived in the small Italian village they had grown up in as children. Approaching the world without a formal education after high school was well within the norm of what they knew and was part of their paradigm. Competing in what is a cutthroat business culture in the United States without the benefits of this education was terrifying. I was determined to be more than the man my father was or whom he saw me as. I made it so much my goal to succeed that I had my own business and employees by the time I was twenty- one, as proof against all of those who did NOT believe I could do it!

Another example of how determined I was, I could remember that as a young man, I have always envisioned and then created exactly what it was that I wanted. As a teen, I wanted beautifully designed clothes and we clearly did not have the money to afford them. My mother had a sewing machine so I set out to get them made. I hired skilled people to make clothing and, in turn, I would sell the finished garments to others. A tailor hired me and I simply subcontracted the work out never doing much of the actual work. This was my very first lucrative venture. I eventually learned that I was able to "deconstruct" garments and then create a pattern and make them for commerce. Needless to say, I was the best-dressed student in my school.

In addition to my sense of visual design and creativity, I love art and have studied artists like Michelangelo and Leonardo da Vinci as well as their works. Wanting the skill for myself, I set out to study and purchase books on how these skills are learned. I quickly started sketching with a pencil to visualize my dreams. Knowing full well that this was a door to source. The first step, which I unwittingly discovered is that it, is important to write and visualize. Later I became fascinated with technology, another amazing tool! I just had to have it and understand it. People who know me today know that I am a techie, always interested and making sense of the latest techno gadget or tool. I was in middle school when I had saved enough money to buy an Atari system. Now this was not a gaming system, rather it was a programmable computer. It was among the first that made it into people's homes even before the PC or Apple were out. Now, as I stated before, my parents were more of the old school mindset of immigrants and a tool like this one was incomprehensible, let alone something that their son should waste his time and money on. The cost of this was prohibitive so, while I had this amazing tool to play with and program, I had to keep it in the box and hide it underneath my bed completely hidden from my parents. There was a certainly beautiful guilty pleasure in knowing I had it and was able to make it work, but I mastered it secretly and made it function. Needless to say, even though I had to work on it alone, and in isolation, I was not about to give up on what I saw as an important part of my future.

As I stated earlier, my parents had a business, and I was never genuinely encouraged to pursue an education at the university level. While this frustrated me because many of my friends went off to college after high school, I was determined to earn the money to create my life and actualize all the things that I envisioned. I opened my own brick and mortar business at age 21, without the guidance or experience of the average businessman. Again, self-taught, I had studied franchise businesses and how they worked and sought to model my business after them, rather than the predictable mom and pop businesses that were and are increasingly becoming a dying breed. I was able to successfully open my first store, followed by eight others, and am still running a successful one to this day!

One of the unforeseen benefits that I had from creating my own business was the fact that I have been able to employ thousands of people over the years. By employing them, I have also developed the ability to interview and listen to people. My instincts and intuition have developed and enabled me to read people incredibly well. I am also very open and honest when I work with people. I have typically trusted people to behave the way that I do, honestly and as a man of my words. I have hired people who have gone on to create their own businesses and develop and know their own purpose. I have been a vehicle to help many others achieve while I have continued on the journey to discover my own purpose and way. This kind of opportunity is not one that I had initially envisioned, but as I reflect back on what I saw for myself, I am proud of how I have made such a positive impact and influence in the lives of the many men and women who have worked for me over the years. This kind of legacy is powerful.

So I have shared with you the way I thought I was being successful and I truly believed in it. Later on in life, during my real estate career, I was attracting successes. I had not read or become familiar with Napoleon Hill's works, yet but I was continuing to benefit from what he had observed and documented in his work. I know in retrospect that my favorite chapter, "Persistence," is the one, which has kept me on task and profiting all these years. As a real estate agent, I learned from a friend about a real estate agency that enables its agents to keep a larger percentage of the commissions on each sale. This fascinated me; as I was already involved personally with the purchase of various pieces of real estate (starting at age sixteen by finding properties in the Classifieds). She introduced me to this group, which fostered the development of the individual and skills. It was through this group that I then became aware of professional development workshops, which could enhance my selling skills. As adept as I am, there are key elements that I became introduced to and embraced which helped me create a more powerful and in-flow business. I was able to attract clients to me who understood who I am and what I could offer them. This subsequently resulted in selling an amazing amount of real estate in my first year. Attending workshops and conferences on Sales with the likes of Mike Ferry and Brian Tracy taught me a tremendous amount. As I have continued to research and study in the years since then, I see and understand where and how these men were inspired and have continued reading and learning things that influence me even now.

The business that I opened at age twenty- one is where I have acquired developed and polished the skills that I use artfully on a daily basis. At that young age, I believe I was more about ego and determination, backed by skills and indefatigable energy, to achieve what so many others said I definitely would NOT! I researched and studied how to make my business not just state of the art, but a trendsetter, at least in the area where I lived. The businesses in my area are typically and traditionally mom and pop brick and mortar types. I was determined to make my business stand out in every way possible - from the ways in which my products were produced to home delivery, as well as marketing and advertising! No one in the area was even thinking in the way that I was thinking. They all thought I was crazy!

I had, by then, purchased an Apple computer and the necessary software to allow me to create my vision and then have it materialize before me. Long before the internet presented all of us with amazing How to videos on YouTube or through Google, I was faced with the need, the intelligence and the burning desire to get things done. I researched the old school way by reading magazines and books in order to actually decide on the Apple for my work. The Atari hidden from my parents was genuine inspiration for the work I set out to do. I studied what kinds of advertising were attractive and how larger businesses were choosing to market their products. I loved pouring over the advertisements and layouts in full color magazines for inspiration and ideas of how to co-opt a style and have it work in my advertising. Design and layout became second nature to me. It was a baptism by fire since there are no tutorials to follow and even those that came with the programs were limited and did not create the advanced pieces I saw in my mind. Within months, I was producing increasingly more professional pieces, having others in the trade asking who was doing my work. My pride allowed me to tell them it was me. Other businesses in the area started contacting me to do their advertising for them. I branched out, not just to complete the layout, copy editing and logo designs, but also to working directly with printers to produce and mail their advertisements for them. My need to efficiently complete my own advertising branched out into another lucrative source of income for me. I was able to be completely involved with elements of the things I loved; art, design, and creativity while I continued with my brick and mortar business that I entrusted others to capably run for me. I am constantly improving my skills in areas as they grow. The marketplace is still a playground!

The progress of my life and business has not always been as straightforward as I would have hoped. I have been blessed by the byproducts of tragic disadvantages for the area I live in. In 2013, Hurricane Sandy came in and truly decimated the region. I had limited damage at my personal home, but I am witness to people in my neighborhood and area who are still struggling to return to homes almost three years later. My business was minimally affected by the storm and I immediately saw an opportunity, not to price gouge, but to provide for the people in my area. The morning after the storm, my family and I were able to bring hot food to first responders in the area as well as people struggling in their yards to clear themselves out from under the debris. It was the right thing to do, my family and business were able to provide, so that is exactly what we did. I was able, for several months afterwards, to continue to provide warm meals for anyone who came to us and was in need. I look back on that and know that the success I had is one of the heart. I still have people and customers come in and share with me their many stories of survival and gratitude for what I was able to help to provide for them in a dark time of need, when even the state was slow to help. I have and will always be true to myself and follow the principles of the heart.

I learned early, without the names or labels for it, that the law of attraction, law of vibration, whatever words a person applies to it, is present and undeniably there. Being able to become and stay attuned is the beautiful challenge we are all faced with daily. I am reflecting on what it is that I can share that demonstrates and illustrates what my journey has been and , still is. It is certainly far from over. As I sit here writing, I am happy and grateful that I am achieving one of my goals right this moment by writing a chapter for this book! I feel as though I have been seeking and taking advantage of opportunities and working towards my goals my entire life. Still, each day as I awake, I recognize that I have a challenge ahead of me again! Every day brings with it the unique possibilities, opportunities and challenges of the day before and then some I have yet to notice or define. I am not fearful, instead I take a breath and look at how I have gotten here, listening to the universe and then make a plan to move on. It is then that I am reminded of what I have learned specifically from Napoleon Hill's formative classic, Think and Grow Rich. It is Chapter Nine, "Persistence" which has guided me through my businesses, personal successes and LIFE. While I find great value in the entire book, it is the ideas and the meaning of this specific chapter that have enabled me to progress, succeed and continue to grow. If I do not plant seeds and grow, then I will never be able to harvest what I have sown. If I cannot do that, then why bother doing anything?

I know that I must persist. Unfortunately, the people around us are always not in a true and harmonious vibration; they cannot be or everyone would be having the same results. Everyone would be wealthy and healthy and they would also be available to help each of us reach our goals. This sympathetic and energized ideal world is simply not true at this time. No one is placed on this planet to help anyone else. A child is helpless during its first days of life and pretty much for many years of its life. We cannot go into the wild and protect ourselves, nor can we feed or shelter ourselves. As children we desperately need the assistance of someone who will, out of the kindness of his heart, help us. Or is this the case? Children trust their parents and families to protect them and care for them. Sometimes, unfortunately that trust is breached. Are people simply caring out of kindness? I think not. I think that this understanding of trust and caring is a process that we soon have to realize so we can realize that TRUST can be misused and our own growth may cease to be. It is a delicate balance that too many of us do unconsciously, following the paradigm and patterns of our parents, our culture. We need to become, to be aware.

Beginning life and being dependent upon another, rather than discovering and pursuing one's own purpose is the easy, complacent way to continue. Those first sparks of interests and conscious desires of youth need to be fed and fanned, not squelched, hidden or put out. Ours is a world where the paradigms and patterns that have been established for keeping everyone in line are the ones that indeed can keep us from or delay us from realizing our purpose in this world. The idea of realizing our purpose is put on a pedestal for us theoretically by schools and families, yet any of us who seek to branch out and go onto to that unbeaten or unfamiliar path in its pursuit are held back or fed their fears. EVERY person has to trust his or her inner purpose and calling as soon as it makes itself heard. It will speak to each of us relatively soon in life. It is a person's obligation to listen and to trust the inner voice when it appears. It would be a beautiful process if the ones who cared for us let us be ourselves from the very start. Too many are caught in the habits of their fathers, mothers and teachers. If at the first sign

136

of the voice coming alive in our hearts we would be encouraged and fed the love that we need to recognize and pursue our purpose that is what a genuine journey to success is. Too many of us come to discover this ideal, as we are older. As difficult as it is, we must learn to trust no one until you listen to that voice speaking directly to you. When you hear the voice and recognize yourself and your purpose, then you can enjoy the journey.

As I reflect on what I have written so far, I have come to realize at the age of 50 that all this is meaningless without one thing, Purpose. You will find yourself frustrated, as I was all my life chasing and trying to recognize and find my purpose. Without joy and purpose you might as well jump off a building or at least come to understand what makes a person even consider doing that. It is at that point of "A-HA ...this is what I should have been doing!", when you can envision yourself completely alive and not dying, that you can create and activate the purpose that seems to have been lying too long in the shadows, waiting to be courted and brought to the forefront. Knowing and acting on your life's purpose is paramount and any shortcut you take, any compromise you make, is completely foolish. Delaying it can be a cause for sadness and for a person who is not accustomed to the discipline of persistence, it might make it easier to never truly pursue it. That would be truly sad. I should know. I also know that it is never too late to change and look ahead. Things are just what they appear to be, illusions and drawings into the sky. We paint our lives, as we desire them and we conjure patterns and situations of thoughts.

As I write this, I reflect on one of the darkest financial moments of my life, which has filled me with fear. I took a risk and I am being tested greatly by the Universe, though I believe myself to be unshaken by this temporary defeat. I am responsible for how I think and I choose the destiny I want to create. I have noticed love come pouring in from friends just reaching out randomly, kind gestures from people and the bright sunshine I notice now. I realize with every venture that I may lose everything that I have worked so hard for and no amount of determination can make it like I may simply envision it. I have even cried and felt like I have lost a slight bit of hope, even blaming myself for the choices that I made. Fear has consumed me. I grasped it and observe it and say willingly that I can choose my own outcome. I am eager to love life; To love people; To believe. As quickly as I shift my mindset another yet more intriguing opportunity appears and speaks to me. This is without question a blessing from SOURCE. I truly believe and love the people who are important to me. I send you love.

Becoming attuned to the vibration within ourselves, as we recognize the intent and meaning of our purpose and what we value, is a strong beginning. Is it a secret? No, but the obvious and true has always been around us and we often have not recognized those beautiful things, taking them too long for granted. Our purpose, our journey, our success at living and understanding our purpose, in the small ways we interact in this world, as well as our purpose as one of the many, one of the spirit, that is what we need to recognize and celebrate. It takes being awake, and our current culture seems to want us to be sleepwalkers. A journey by a sleepwalker will not get us far and indeed can lead us to injury. It's a challenge to realize one's awakening. It's downright frightening to look into that cosmic mirror, that spiritual reflection and see who is looking back. But just wait until you see who IS looking back at you! You may not immediately recognize the face, but the spirit, yes. No journey is the same, even when people are walking hand in hand, but each of us, each of our spirits can and must be free. Looking at the purpose and sensibilities of this book, I realize that I have wandered (eyes wide open) and see that every Journey to Success can be summed up in one value, in one word, and that is BE. Be yourself!

BIO

Tony Fevola, Entrepreneur and Branding Innovator

Tony Fevola is a successful businessman who has 30 years experience and worked in all areas of businesses, from starting several successful brick and mortar stores, developing marketing and growing sales for each of them to consulting others in their fields. He has had the opportunity to work in sales achieving awards for his productivity and success. He has been an investor and developer in several companies. He has coached and consulted others on how to develop and grow their own businesses. He has created merchant websites and brand developing. He now utilizes his vast experiences and knowledge to consult and creatively market for his clients.

You can reach him by email: tonyfevola@gmail.com

MAKE YOUR LIFE A MASTERPIECE
By: Ana C Fontes

Life's Purpose

The World has a population of more than seven billion people living on different continents, speaking different languages, and experiencing different things all the time. About 350,000 babies are born every day in the world. They will grow up and become adults with desires; goals and frustrations just like all of us. Some of them will become leaders, winners, doers and others will become followers, quitters, and procrastinators. The first group will focus on their life's purpose, keeping a positive mental attitude and always going the extra mile to fight for the life they desire to have. These people see opportunities in every obstacle they face. They see failure as a temporary defeat, and they never avoid the opportunity to learn from it. The second group of people will just accept life as if they have no control over it. They will be dominated by fear and negative thoughts hoping things will get better someday.

In which group of people would you classify yourself? Have you ever wondered why some people seem to be so happy and accomplished in life while others seem to always be struggling to find their way? The good news is it does not matter, which group you fit in, or where you are in life right now. What matters is where you want to go. Most people do not even know what their life's purpose is. Those people just react to what happens to them. If that is your case, stop and dedicate some time to finding out what your life's purpose is. It's never too late to fight for the life you always dreamed about. You can start changing your life right now. Don't ask yourself how long it will take; ask how far you can go. Being a good observer is key in life. I think parents should teach their kids about the importance of this skill. It gives us the ability to learn from other people's experience.

Life is rich and so interesting! My mom always said that LIFE is the best teacher in the world, and I completely agree with her. Life is a like a restless teacher. We are constantly either teaching or learning, even if we do not realize it. Unfortunately, some people do not even learn from their own experiences, even less from other people's experiences. These people get stuck in life, and they blame it on somebody else. We are very creative in finding excuses to not change our lives. Do not make excuses; make results. We all have areas in our lives where we wish we were better. Wishing is not enough. We need to have a burning desire to change and improve. We should embrace changes in all aspects of our life.

"10% of your attitude is determined by what life hands to you and 90% is how you choose to respond."
- Charles Swindoll

Enthusiasm is Key to your Life's Transformation

My mom is my role model. If I had to describe my mom in only one word, it would be "enthusiastic". I learned from her since I was very little to look at life with positivism and enthusiasm. She always sees the bright side in a dark situation and she always believes there is a solution to every problem. When my brother was in his early thirties, he was diagnosed with a brain tumor. It was a rare type of cancer that is more common in little kids and at that time, there were only a few cases of that kind, so doctors were not very sure about his chances of surviving.

I remember as if it was yesterday when we were at the hospital nervously waiting for my brother's surgery to finish. We were desperate because it was a very delicate surgery and my mom, in a very calm tone of voice, told us to calm down and be confident. She said she had no doubt he would make it. She knew her son was a warrior ever since the moment he

141

was born. He had complications at birth and fought for his life when the doctors did not have hope he would make it. Thank God my mom was right once again. My brother took this battle very seriously and focused on his recovery one step at a time. Thanks to his positive mental attitude, faith, determination and enthusiasm for life, he won this battle. He is like my mom; he is full of life. He puts passion into everything he does. His energy is contagious.

He is one of those people that you feel good to be around, just like my dad was. He has a beautiful and pure smile. I am sure he does not take his life for granted, and that is how we all should be. We need to be thankful for all we have, thankful for being alive. Most people focus on what they do not have instead of been thankful for what they already have. That is a big mistake, and it will hold you back from reaching your goals. Did you ever think that some people did not wake up this morning? 150,000 people die every day in the world. If you woke up breathing this morning, you should be thankful. Do not be a spectator of your own life. Do not allow it to just pass by. Search inside your soul to find out your life's purpose and never lose focus on it. Not having a life purpose is like taking a plane without knowing its destiny. You don't know where you will end up.

My mom loves to sew. Gardening and sewing are her favorite hobbies. She used to spend hours per day at the sewing machine making beautiful clothes for us when we were little. One day when I was fifteen, I was trying on a beautiful dress she had just made for me when she noticed something was not right. One side of the dress was not aligned on my shoulder. So, she went to fix the dress, and she realized the dress was perfect, the problem was with my shoulders. One was lower than the other one. My parents then decided to take me to a famous orthopedist in the big city of São Paulo to check my spine. This doctor was my dad's professor at the medical school in São Paulo. My dad admired him very much, and he had no doubt that he would be the best doctor to go. That was when we learned I had Scoliosis; my spine has a little curve instead of being straight.

142

Exactly a month later, I lost one of the most important people in my life: my wonderful and unforgettable dad. He suddenly passed away from a fatal heart attack at the age of 46. How devastating! What a tragedy! We see things like this happening in other families, but we never think it will happen to us. I could never imagine life without him. Life made no sense at that moment. My mom was left with two teenagers and a ten-year-old girl. My mom is the strongest person I have ever met. She is my Hero with a capital "H"! She taught us to become stronger from this horrible tragedy. My mom made us believe that life would be good again and that we could still be happy even without having dad there. We could feel the power that a family has together. She always says there is no limit where there is love, faith and belief!

"Every adversity, every failure and every hard-ache carries with it a seed of an equivalent or greater benefit".
-Napoleon Hill

Back to the story, when I went back to the doctor for the follow-up appointment a month after the first visit, the doctor was double shocked. First, because he did not know my dad had passed way. Second, he was so surprised to see that my spine's curve got a lot worse in a matter of days, in literally less than a month. Why did it happen? How was it possible? According to him, there are a few things that can cause it to happen and growing up too fast and experiencing a major trauma are two of them. The trauma and the pain of losing my dad did that to my spine. That's how powerful our mind is! Now I understand that I allowed my sadness and negative thoughts during that tragedy to cause all that in my body! I wish I knew back then what I know today about the power of the mind and the power of positive thinking. It was a huge lesson for me, and I learned to stay alert and always monitor my thoughts.

143

*"There's no limitations to your mind, except those
we acknowledge"*
- Napoleon Hill

Embrace Changes

The only thing that never changes is change itself

Change is a word that scares most people. It never scared me. I always, and I mean always, think about opportunities that will come with "changes". You will think that I am crazy with my next statement, but that is how I am. I love to move to a new house, new city or to a new country! I feel very inspired and motivated when I have a new place to explore or a new language to learn. I love not knowing what is around me and having to figure out everything again. The "unknown" sounds very attractive and motivating to me. You know what I do when things get a little boring at home? If you ask this question to my husband or my kids, I am sure they will have the answer right away for you.

I love to move furniture around just to change things up. This is a big sign that I am bored so I need to provoke some changes in my life even if it is just furniture rearrangement. I am not talking about buying new furniture. I am talking about moving furniture around, creating new spaces and a new look with the same stuff. I do that every once in a while, and it makes me feel very good. When my husband catches me standing in the corner of a room in our house, staring at the furniture, he says: "Please don't come up with new ideas! I know what you are thinking. You want to move some furniture around! Everything looks great. There's no need to change anything!" Then I know he is not in the mood for changes. So, I don't say anything. I just wait for him to go to work, and the kids to go to school, and I move everything by myself.

Most the time I do not get it right the first time, but I keep trying and voilà! I have a new room! It is such a great feeling. At the end of the day when they come back home, they always have a good surprise and usually their comment is something like: "Wow! It looks so much better! Why didn't we think about it before?" It looks like a new house but in reality, nothing is new. Then I always say: "We need to keep challenging ourselves to renovate, to innovate, to be creative, to do something different every day. I thought it would look better but I would not know for sure until I tried it", and that is what life is about. We need to use our creativity and try new things. They will open our minds to new possibilities we never thought of before, and the reward we get is the great feeling that comes with it. Do not be afraid of changes because many times they will bring great opportunities to you.

"If you want to have more,
you have to become more.
For things to improve, you have to improve.
For things to change, you have to change.
When you change, everything changes for your".
- Jim Rohn

Stop reading right now and make a list of ten things you would like to do that you have never done before. Prioritize your list and take action! Do not give yourself a chance to regret things you did not do. There is only one person that can change your life: YOU!

Be Bigger than Your Problems

Practice creative vision

You know those stories that open your eyes or at least make you rethink of how you do things? A long time ago I read an interesting story that always comes to my mind when I face a tough situation. Unfortunately, I cannot recall the name of the book or the article where I read it but it's a well-known story sited in many sources. I like this story so much that I tell it in my book, and I think it is worth repeating it here. I am sure it will also make you rethink how you react to some situations the same way it did to me. This story reinforces the power of creative vision and creative thinking.

In the early 1910s, there was a farmer that had a little land and he used to work very hard to put food on the table for his family. One day his orchard caught fire, and all the fruits and vegetables were burned. He was desperate because he had no way to take care of his family. So, he decided to take a loan from a bank in the closest city. He took the money from the bank and rebuilt everything. Then a devastating thunderstorm came, and he lost all his fruits and vegetables for the second time. He had no money to pay the bank back. At that time, somebody that could not pay a bank loan would go to jail.

Desperate, he decided to talk to the lender to see if together they could find a solution. The lender told him he had a proposal to make, but he would need to come back the day after and bring his beautiful daughter with him. The farmer did not like the fact he asked him to bring his daughter, but he had no other option. So, the next day the farmer and his daughter came to the bank to talk to the lender. The farmer said: "So, what do you have to propose? You know I have no money to pay you."

The lender looked at the floor. The floor had lots of blue and green pebbles as decoration. Then he said: "There is a bunch of blue and green pebbles on the floor. I will pick one of each. I have two bags in my hands, and I'll put a blue pebble in a bag and a green one in the other bag. I will pick a color and then your daughter will guess which bag has a pebble with that color. If she guesses right, you two can go home, and your loan is paid off but if she guesses wrong, she stays with me, and you go home. She will be the payment. The farmer did not know what to do since obviously he did not want to lose his daughter, but he also did not want to go to jail. His daughter noticed that the lender was cheating when he put a blue pebble in both bags. He said: I want you to guess which bag has the green pebble. If you pick the

146

right one your dad does not need to pay the loan and you go home with him, but if you pick the wrong one, you are mine.

The girl was in shock and did not know what to do since she knew she could not pick a green pebble. Her dad told her that he would rather go to jail because he could not give her as payment of his loan. She almost agreed with him because she knew they could not win since there was no green pebble in any of the bags. She thought about fighting with the lender telling him that he was cheating but at the same time, she knew that it would not solve the problem. At that moment, she felt challenged to find a creative way to win that situation without letting the lender know she knew he was cheating.

The pressure of the moment was all she needed to use her creativity. Suddenly, a great idea came to her mind. She told the lender that they would accept his proposal. She could see in the lender's face how happy he was because he knew she could not win. Her dad was in shock and desperate. He had no idea his daughter had a good plan. Then she picked one bag from the lender's hands and put her hand inside to get the pebble. When she was taking the pebble out of the bag she "accidentally" dropped the pebble on the floor very quickly. It got mixed up with all the others which made it impossible to know which one she had picked so the lender said: "We will need to do it all over again since there is no way to know which one you dropped".

She was ready and waiting for that comment, and she said right away: "No, sir. It is easy! All we need to do is to check what color is in the other bag. And since we had a blue pebble in one bag and a green one in the other bag, that will tell us if I picked the right one or not. I picked the wrong one if the one inside of the bag in your hand is green or I picked the right one if it is blue." The lender had no other option than opening the bag and showing them the pebble. Of course, it was a blue pebble, and the farmer and his daughter went home happy.

Many times, we need to think different than most people think. The farmer's daughter saved his life. Great achievements involve great risk. She converted that risky situation into a great opportunity. The pebble game that seemed to be very dangerous for the farmer ended up being the opportunity to solve his problem. You need to change the way you think, and you will discover opportunities. Usually, those opportunities are hidden to most people's eyes. Some opportunities require courage and risk-taking and if you are not willing to do that, you will probably see them as obstacles.

Next time you face an obstacle remember the farmer's daughter story and look for the opportunity hidden in it. Take time to figure it out. Always challenge yourself to practice creative thinking. I guarantee that you will be very surprised with the great things that will happen in your life. If you practice it every time an obstacle comes up your way, you will get used to it and the more you get used to it the better your life will be. You will also realize that you have the power to change your life. Use adversity to your advantage.

Do what you love. Find your life's purpose and build a plan to reach it!

Embrace obstacles and be ready for opportunities!

The Lion, the Gazelle and You

Practice creative vision

I read the Lion and the Gazelle fable a long time ago, and I never forget it. I think it is worth mentioning this story here even if you have already heard it. Every day in Africa a gazelle wakes up knowing that it must run faster than the fastest lion otherwise it will be killed. Every day a lion wakes up, and it knows it must outrun the slowest gazelle, or it will starve to death. The moral of the story is that both will need to start running as soon as the sun comes up.

Following this fable, I read an interesting story about two executives that went to Africa on a safari. They woke up the first day very excited, got all the equipment, riffles, binoculars and guides and went out for a very fun day. They were so excited during the safari that they did not notice they got too far from where they were camping. Suddenly a huge lion started chasing them. They did not have the riffles ready yet so the only thing they could do was run as fast as they could. The lion was getting closer and closer to them. Then one of them who was very tired and almost ready to give up said: "*It does not matter how fast we run, the lion will get us. I watched a documentary that said lions are much faster than humans*". Then the other executive said: *Who said I'm worried about running faster than the lion? All I need to do is run faster than you!*"

I thought I would mention this story not to discuss friendship since it certainly would not be a good one. The reason I like this story is because it illustrates very well the importance of a positive mental attitude and focus. In a difficult situation most people would try to find a solution for a little while but then fear comes and dominates them allowing the problem to become bigger than them, and when that happens, it becomes impossible to find a solution. A positive mental attitude and creative thinking are the two important pieces in this story. I do not even think this is a true story, but it is a great story to make us rethink how we face obstacles.

The lion represents many things in our lives. We face lions every day, and our destinies depend on how we react to them. Many times we give up too soon, and we miss a big opportunity because we focus on the wrong thing. We need to believe in ourselves. Like James L. Oleson said: "People doubt their beliefs and believe their doubts. Believe in yourself and the world will believe in you".

Be the creator of your own life and do not allow other people to hold you back. Learn to convert obstacles into opportunities. Discover your "why" and focus on your life's purpose. Be the change you want to see in your life. There is no better time to start than now! Get prepared because great things will happen to you!

> *"I never made one of my discoveries through the process of rational thinking"*
> -Albert Einstein

Every day I remind myself to use my ears to listen to my intuition, my eyes to see the hidden opportunities, my mind to empower me to face any situation and my heart to remind me that feelings become thoughts, and thoughts become things.

I hope my stories inspire you the same way they do to me. There is no secret. Do not live a limited life. Embrace it! Improve it! Change it! You get what you spend time doing. Practice creative vision, add enthusiasm in all you do, embrace changes, never give up and get ready for the big transformation. You are the creator of your own life. Focus on your life's purpose and make it a masterpiece! Do it right now, because this is the only NOW you have.

BIO

Ana C Fontes was born and raised in Brazil. In 1999, she moved to the US with her husband and their two kids. They became American citizens a few years later. Ana's passion to learn about different cultures and countries guided her to do what she does today. Her cross-cultural business expertise spans 27 years in marketing and international business development. She has worked in Latin America, the US, Europe, and China and has held executive leadership positions for multi-national companies.

Ana lives in Texas, USA and considers herself a fortunate person because she does what she loves. She works with people from different cultures and companies around the globe, helping them to find opportunities to expand their businesses. In her personal life, she focuses on helping others learn how to turn obstacles into opportunities. She discovered the Napoleon Hill teachings 10 years ago, and it influenced her personal and professional life. Ana joined the Napoleon Hill Foundation in 2014 as a student. She is a co-author of the book Beyond What If - Real Life Stories on how Purpose Turns Dreams into Reality by the Napoleon Hill's Certified Instructors and Students.

Ana loves to receive messages from readers with their life stories.

Contact Ana at anafontes@anafontes.com

Check out Ana's BLOG at www.anafontes.com for more inspiring stories.

Ana's main message is:
"See opportunities where others see obstacles."

FOREVER A STUDENT
By: Craig Kulesa

"Always do what you are afraid to do"
-Ralph Waldo Emerson

Napoleon Hill said it best: The Master Key is intangible, but it is powerful! It is the privilege of creating, in your own mind, a burning desire for a definite form of riches. There is no penalty for the use of the key but there is a price you must pay if you do not use it. The price is failure. There is a reward of stupendous proportions if you put the key to use. It is the satisfaction that comes to all who conquer self and force life to pay whatever is asked.

A Life Lesson at 14,000 Feet

My life played out before me; all my choices, experiences, and the ones I might never get to have. As the plane took off I was beginning to question my own judgment. This was real Fear; a life or death situation. Either I would live to tell the tale of jumping out of an airplane or I would end up as fertilizer. The day before was my 35th birthday and this was all part of the plan. While I was surrounded by other brave souls ready to jump, I was alone. I did not even tell my parents; I knew that they would be concerned for my safety and their fear would not help me. My mission: to conquer my fears, one by one, so I could move forward on my journey to self-mastery.

The plane climbed in altitude and the instructor provided some last minute tips. Everything depended on how well he packed the parachute. We went into a slight nosedive to create a semi-weightless environment, allowing us to maneuver to the open door. One by one, people started disappearing from the open door. The sound of the engines and rushing wind was deafening. I had to remind myself to breathe while putting my faith into something greater than me. Through the noise I heard him yell 3! – 2! - 1!

Planting Seeds

Flash back to 1990 in Connecticut; I was 12 years old, the movie Home Alone was a hit, The Simpsons aired for the first time, and Operation Desert Shield began. My parents worked hard to provide a life for me that they never enjoyed. I remember it vividly; my father surprised me with a gift. This gift would forever change my life although it would be years before I would ever know it. It was an audiobook cassette version of Think and Grow Rich by Napoleon Hill read by Earl Nightingale. Napoleon Hill said, "The oak sleeps in the acorn. The bird waits in the egg, and in the highest vision of the soul, a waking angel stirs."

My father, familiar with the book, suggested that I listen to the audio every night as I went to bed. He explained that the principles of success would become a part of my subconscious mind as I slept. I followed his advice and enjoyed hearing the stories of successful people like Thomas Edison and Henry Ford as I drifted to sleep. This would be the beginning of my understanding of the power of the subconscious mind.

I did not have a definite purpose despite listening to Think and Grow Rich. I followed the natural path that life was presenting me. Unknowingly, I was neglecting to exercise the privilege Napoleon Hill described, casting myself upon the broad sea of Circumstance where I would be tossed around like a ship without a rudder on the waves of the ocean.

As the next few years went by, I got my first job at a pet supply store and later a sales job at a national retailer. Determined to work hard and get a head start on life, I quickly got a second job as an auto parts salesperson. I loved working on cars with my father and by the time I was ready for my driver's license, I helped fix up my first car.

It was my junior year in high school and I fell in love for the first time in my life; letting my emotions guide my decisions. The more I wanted to be with my girlfriend, the more my grades slipped, and the more my parents grew concerned. It was expected of me to go to college, but my emotions convinced me that my relationship was a priority. It would be the beginning of my lifelong task to find a balance between my emotions and reason.

Once I graduated high school, I got a third job stocking shelves at a local grocery store at night. Tensions escaladed with my parents, however, I was sure of my desire and no one was going to tell me what to do. I made the decision to follow my girlfriend to Arkansas and left my home and family behind.

"If you do not conquer self,
you will be conquered by self"
-Napoleon Hill

Definiteness of purpose is the starting point of all achievement. It is the stumbling block of 98% of all people because they never really define their goals and definite plans for their achievement. I finally had goals and definite plans; I would do whatever it took to make a good life for my loved ones and I. Albeit; my goals were mostly materialistic and measured in dollars and a standard of living.

Just a Mechanic

I wanted freedom, to make lots of money, travel, and have a successful life. I found myself in a totally foreign environment without anything but my dreams. At the time, my plan was to become a truck driver; I would get paid to travel the country. To make ends meet, I started a job with the same retail company that I had worked for during high school.

Every journey starts with the first step and I vowed to have the ambition to start making life pay off on my own terms. After realizing the difficulties in getting a driving job and maintaining a relationship, my focus turned to being a diesel mechanic. I was always fascinated by heavy equipment and already had experience repairing cars. Through this experience, I discovered one of my gifts is troubleshooting repairs plus, I enjoyed the challenge. With no experience I started at the bottom to work my way up. With persistence (I kept checking back with the service manager until he hired me), I landed an apprentice job at minimum wage repairing tractors and construction equipment.

I had a goal of becoming an ASE Master Certified Technician in the field and within 5 years I had reached my goal. To top it off, I managed to get my CDL to drive commercial trucks. During this time, I was working two jobs, living in a mobile home and still not satisfied with where I was.

Catching the Real Estate Bug

I started to realize that being a diesel mechanic was not going to get me to the kind of life I desired financially or other wise. Somehow, the idea of making a business out of real estate appealed to me. I signed up for real estate classes at my local community college and began classes in between my other two jobs. It was at this point that I met a real estate agent who would become a friend of mine for years to come. He mentioned that I should read a book called Rich Dad, Poor Dad by Robert Kiyosaki. It inspired me so much that I began immediately to make plans to build my real estate business.

Napoleon Hill says that definiteness of purpose can be described as pursuing the work for that which you are best fitted with a definite object to strive for. Real estate was an obsession for me; it meant freedom and unlimited potential. I began buying vacant properties for resale and investment with my hard earned money. Eventually, I started buying single-family homes, fixing them up and renting them. Soon after, I realized developing property would create more equity, so I built my business around that.

All the time, I was working both jobs, as a mechanic during the day and retail on nights and weekends. It was hard work but it did not seem like work because I loved what I did. The best part was creating affordable housing for families in desirable school districts and managing those properties. I discovered the riches associated with providing valuable service to others while moving in the direction of my dreams.

After years of hard work between two jobs, I was able to quit and start working for myself full time. It was scary and exciting all at the same time; much like the experience of jumping out of an airplane that I would later experience. I realized that the time would never be just right.

The lesson I learned in going out on my own was best described in one of Napoleon Hill's speeches:

"One of Napoleon's (Bonaparte) generals came to him one day as they were fixing to attack the next morning and this general says, 'sir, the circumstances are not just right for the attack tomorrow'

And Napoleon says, 'circumstances my right heel! I make circumstances! Attack!!

And I have never seen a successful man yet in any business that didn't say when somebody says it can't be done – he said Attack! Attack!

Start where you are, and when you get around the curve in the road you'll know you can't see by it till you get there – you'll always find that the road goes on around!

Attack!

Don't procrastinate! Don't stand still! Attack!"

Think and Grow Rich Rediscovered

All ideas begin as the result of definiteness of purpose; I would come to fully understand this when I rediscovered Think and Grow Rich as an adult. In my quest to keep expanding my business and investments, I started investing in the Foreign Exchange Market. Things went really well for a while, but in a blink of an eye I ended up losing everything I had. It was an expensive lesson that knocked me down pretty hard. I decided to never let that happen again. It was a turning point in my life that showed I was on a path for self-destruction, chasing money with no sense of purpose.

It was at this time of self despair that I vowed to put whatever time I had to devote to learning everything I could about business, success, and personal achievement. It resonated so strongly that I set out immediately to acquire as much knowledge as possible. That is when Napoleon Hill's work appeared before me as if by something greater than chance. This time I would not be able to put that book down. I read it once, and later lost count how many times. I bought the audio version where I listened to it innumerable times; mowing the grass, driving to work, and as much as I could at other times.

I was so serious about ingraining the principles of success into my mind that I rewrote the entire book covering about 2 pages a day. An interesting thing started to happen; I started getting ideas that popped into my head like flashes of inspiration. I took the words of Napoleon Hill and treated them with the utmost respect. I realized that I was receiving ideas that were not necessarily generated from my own mind. The excitement from this experience fueled me to dive more in to my quest for self-development. I finally developed my definiteness of purpose for enduring success; to conquer one's self is the only lasting goal worth any amount of time or resource.

They Told Me So

The time had come to admit that my parents were right to want me to go to college. However, an important point here was my willingness and desire. If I went to college just to satisfy someone else's desire it would not have been as meaningful or beneficial as me doing it on my own direction. I attended an accredited college online that would allow me to run my business during the day and study when I was not working. This journey would not be easy or cheap, but I had to do it and the time was right.

All Good Things...

My goals and my quest to improve myself were definite and nothing was going to change that, but I was not the only one going through change. During my growth I began to see things in my personal life that were not consistent with the way I perceived them before. I remember reading a book in one of my first college classes called Critical Thinking that felt as if it was written specifically for me. There was no denying what I had been discovering and I began questioning my relationship. For the next two years I continued to work on college work and self-development. Finally, after years of being together with the same woman and seeing several professional counselors, we no longer could make the relationship work. It was a tough lesson in love and life; best summed up by Hill;

"One who has loved truly, can never lose entirely.
Love is whimsical and temperamental.
Its nature is ephemeral, and transitory.
It comes when it pleases, and goes away without
warning.
Accept and enjoy it while it remains, but spend no
time worrying about its departure.
Worry will never bring it back."

Thinking will not overcome fear but action will"
- W. Clement Stone

When pursuing your definiteness of purpose, you must be the kind of person that will not settle with life for anything short of what you want. I forced myself to remember that, "every adversity, every failure, every heartbreak, carries with it the seed of an equal or greater benefit."

The Real Enemy

The loss of love is like a death and it felt worse because my identity had been wrapped up in that relationship for 15 years. Not only did I loose my best friend and lover, I did not feel like I knew who I was anymore. I sought professional counseling and by grace I found the perfect counselor for me. My new mission was to feel better about my self, learn about relationships, and continue my self-development to include human connections. The real enemy at hand was exposed and I declared war on it – my fears.

These words gave me hope:
"Remember, too, that all who succeed in life get off to a bad start, and pass through many heartbreaking struggles before they 'arrive'. The turning point in the lives of those who succeed usually comes at some moment of crisis through which they are introduced to their 'other selves'."

New Beginnings

I had never danced in my life, but that would soon change. Not only would learning to dance be therapeutic for me, I would experience human connection and relationships. The toughest dance classes were the first ones.

159

The courage needed just to show up was enormous. I plowed forward and religiously drove 1 hour one-way just to attend classes.

At the same time that I began taking dance classes, my counselor suggested I take up martial arts again. My instinct knew that was the right thing to do and I searched for a local school. In my first Brazilian Jiu Jitsu class, I saw a bunch of guys wrestling on the mats and thought I am not sure I am going to be comfortable doing this. I stayed and can say I never had a workout like that in my life. When I went home that night I threw up and knew immediately that this was something I had to do.

Peace in Chaos

Being present is more important than I ever knew. I never really understood what that term meant or how it applied to life. In my life journey's quest for self-development, I have discovered that the only thing that really matters is the present moment. It relates to Napoleon Hill's teachings and the secret that he spoke so much about. Other teachers have added to my knowledge of this principle including Abraham-Hicks and Eckhart Tolle.

To read and learn about being present is one thing, but to practice it in times of chaos is a totally different experience. I think you come in contact with your other self at these times and you are faced with no choice but to surrender to the moment. Brazilian Jiu Jitsu has been essential for my growth in this skill. You are forced into being present; forced to be at peace with your current situation while thinking of what you can do to create space for options.

With the help of these experiences, I would begin to heal from my past. I managed to make amazing friendships wherever I was and even found love again. Although some of the friendships and lovers have moved on, I am grateful for it all.

Enduring Success and My Purpose

As a fitting climax to this chapter, I would like to share what a brilliant poet accurately stated on this universal truth:

"To laugh often and much
To win the respect of intelligent people and the
affection of children
To earn the appreciation of honest critics
and endure the betrayal of false friends
To appreciate beauty
To find the best in others
To leave the world a bit better, whether by a
healthy child,
a garden patch, or a redeemed social condition
To know even one life has breathed easier because
you have lived
This is to have succeeded."

And as Napoleon Hill advises, "If you must be careless with your possessions, let it be in connection with material things. Your mind is your spiritual state! Protect and use it with the care to which divine royalty is titled. You were given willpower for this purpose."

As I was falling from the plane at terminal velocity, I realized there was no need to fear anymore. All that mattered was that moment; I could choose to enjoy it for all it was or be terrified of an enemy that was invisible. I chose to enjoy the moment. I overcame my fear and my life keeps getting better.

BIO

As an only child, Craig was born and raised in Connecticut. After attending high school, Craig moved to Arkansas & pursued a career in the heavy truck repair industry while earning his ASE Master Medium-Heavy Vehicle repair certification along with a class "A" commercial drivers license. While working truck and tractor dealership and the retail sector, he began taking real estate and business classes at National Park Community College.

In 2002, he founded Sundance Investments Inc., a real estate and property investment company. As president and CEO, he led the company to acquire and develop real assets throughout Arkansas. In 2007, Craig started attending the University of Phoenix online while continuing to expand and manage his company. He would later achieve his Associates in Business, Bachelors of Business Science, and finally his Masters of Business Administration. In addition, he has passed the Napoleon Hill Foundation's online class and attended the certification workshop in Sedona, Arizona in 2013.

As hobbies, Craig is a student of dance and martial arts. He fell in love with both arts at the same time in 2010, where he traveled to Florida to meet and train with his idols for both (Robson Moura for Brazilian Jiu Jitsu & Jorge and Tanja from Island Touch for bachata). He's performed salsa and bachata numerous times throughout Arkansas, Tennessee, Georgia, and Missouri. In addition, he has taught classes, workshops, and choreographies. As a martial arts student in Brazilian Jiu Jitsu, he is currently a purple belt under the 8-time world champion Robson Moura. Building off the

162

fundamentals he learned at Revolution MMA owned and operated by Jory and Abby Malone, he strives to do a little better every class.

Craig can be reached at sundance1331@gmail.com

"RAISE THE BAR AND LIVE YOUR DREAMS"

By: Daniel Zykaj

As I sit here and think about my "Journey to Success" I can't help but reminisce on the ups and downs, the temporary defeats, the challenges and victories that I have faced to get here, all of which have taught me lessons on success. Without realizing it I was applying a lot of the success principles laid out in one of the very first books I ever read on success, "Think and Grow Rich"!

I was born and raised in Albania, a third world country in Eastern Europe. My parents did the best they could to provide a good life for my siblings and I. My mom had a small grocery store and my dad a small welding shop and they worked tirelessly to make it work, but being surrounded by poverty and lack made it very difficult to build a thriving business.

It was my parents dream to one-day move to Greece or Italy or America, anywhere they could become more and have more opportunity. When that chance came in the form of an application to become naturalized US citizens, my parents were among the first to apply. It was a long and arduous process but by the grace of God we were chosen. About 2 years later my parents sold everything they had built and left everything and everyone they knew behind to move to America.

On May 21st 1997 we landed at JFK in New York City and were officially in America on our way to a new home in the suburbs of Detroit Michigan! Moving here was a difficult process and once we got here it was not easy. We faced a new country, culture, and language we did not yet speak.

We lived with my mom's cousin and her family for the first 3 months until my parents could get jobs, find a place to live, and buy a car to get around. The first apartment we could afford was a small 2-bedroom with furniture mostly donated from what little family we had here. The 5 of us now had a home.

My parents went to work almost immediately in a restaurant as dishwashers, and I quickly followed with my first job as a busboy, at just 11 years old. Being the oldest of 3 kids in our culture is a big responsibility. I was expected to help out as much as possible with the household so going to work after school made me feel like I was contributing to the family.

At first I would just go in and help my mom with her job so she could rest, since she went to work at 7 am every day. The man that owned the restaurant was taken back by this action from a kid younger than his own and so after a few months he offered me the bus boy job and I excitedly accepted.

After working in restaurants through my teens, I started to think and speak about owning a restaurant. After graduating from high school I had some money saved for college that I had given my mom to put away for me, but I knew that college was not the path I wanted to take. I wanted to be my own boss and 6 months after graduating from high school in 2005, I became the proud owner of Fraser Coney Island Restaurant on January 16th 2006!

Shortly after becoming a business owner, a customer at the restaurant introduced me to network marketing. I went to a meeting where I met people that had been having tremendous success with the company and I instantly took to it like a fish to water. Long and exhausting 12-hour days at the restaurant did not allow me to pursue network marketing at a very high level. I stayed involved and took a few simple actions, including hosting a few meetings at my home and restaurant and told people about the opportunity and services we offered. I took more interest in the personal development side of the business than the actual business itself. I was introduced to personal development books and audios including Napoleon Hill's "Think and Grow Rich" which stretched my thinking and allowed me to dream bigger. That is really where my journey began.

After reading the books and listening to audios my mind had now been stretched and I understood that there is an exact formula for success. If someone did something admirable, by following the same process they used the results could be duplicated. That single idea has helped propel me to the top of our industry today but it was not easy to get here.

I lacked passion in the first company I was with and just sort of faded out slowly. A few months went by and I stayed out of the network-marketing world by making excuses like not having time and being too busy with my restaurant. Some of the companies I looked at did not excite me but then I was approached by a friend in October of 2011 about a company that sold "healthy coffee" and that is when I went to work in network marketing like never before. For months I talked to people about the opportunity, did the home meetings, hired a new employee at the restaurant to free up time for me to pursue network marketing with the "healthy coffee" company, and shared the products with everyone I knew.

This was what I had been looking for and success started to manifest in small portions at a time. One day we had a big event in Detroit, with one of the top leaders in the company. About eight hundred people attended and when he was done presenting the opportunity he asked who was going to attend the National Convention, which was about 3 weeks away in Dallas, Texas during the Memorial Day weekend of 2012. Everyone cheered and clapped and David was happy with the noisemakers, however he also asked who was not coming. Being honest I raised my hand and almost instantly everyone in the room was staring at me. After looking around I realized that I was the only one in the entire room to raise my hand, and I turned beet red in embarrassment. David asked why I was not going and my answer was that I did not have anyone to cover me at the restaurant, and having to travel for a long weekend just was not in the cards for me at the time. David then said something that blew me away. He told me that in order to build a huge business it was crucial that I attend the big events and if I wanted the results he had I would have to make the sacrifice so my dream could come to pass! David then reached into his pocket and gave me a ticket to the event. I will always remember that moment, because that is when I made the decision to go all in.

Now that the decision was made, I booked the flights and hotel and even talked a few people on my team into going with me. I had committed myself to be in Dallas that weekend even if I had to take a loss and close the restaurant for the weekend.

During this time, I had been planning on remodeling the restaurant and had been taking bids on the remodel. The lowest bid was about $2,500 more than I had budgeted for, and the gentleman that was going to do the job was not willing to negotiate further on the price. When I mentioned that I wanted this done on Memorial weekend he laughed and said there was no way. He had planned that weekend to vacation with his family. Instead, I closed for the extended weekend and gave the days off to my staff.

Two days before I was set to leave for Dallas the gentleman called me and said he was in financial trouble and needed the job to get back on track and not only would he do it for the price I wanted, but he was going to do it during the Memorial Day weekend and it would be completed by the time I returned. Once you make the decision to make your goal and dream come to pass and decide that nothing will get in your way, God or the universe or whatever higher power you believe in will make the circumstances work out and that is the principle of Applied Faith.

I worked with that company for over 2 years and built a team of over 500 representatives by staying consistent, hosting meetings and never missing events. I did that while still working 12-hour days at my restaurant. I wanted more than anything to get to the level that David had achieved. As my business continued to grow I was taking more and more time away from the restaurant. It started to suffer and revenues showed I was clearly at a fork in the road. Even though I was not quite at the level I wanted to be I decided to pursue network-marketing full time. Shortly after making that decision the opportunity to sell the restaurant presented itself. The sale of the restaurant was finalized in May of 2013 and I was now a full time network marketer.

I learned a lot from the activity as well as the books and audios, which had now become part of my daily life and I still felt that something was missing. Sometimes opportunity presents itself in a strange way. I was looking for a mentor in my current company and none appeared. I was invited to a meeting with a group of networkers that were involved in a different company and that is when I came across a legend in the industry.

Bill Hoffmann sat down with me and told me that he would be willing to take me under his wing and teach me everything he had learned over his illustrious 30 years in the industry at the highest levels and income bracket. It took me a few weeks to decide and, after talking it over with a few of the leaders in my team we made the shift and went to work with a new company in the essential services sector.

According to the Mastermind principle you have to surround yourself with people that know things you do not and by having full access to Bill and his specialized knowledge we quickly grew and built a team larger than that in the previous 2 businesses in only 6 months. Things were going great and we were growing daily. Our team had over 4,000 customers and as we continued to build and grow we started to notice that there was a rift with the corporate team, which was coming to a head.

For months we tried our best to help bridge the gap to no avail, and alongside my mentor Bill we decided to move to a new company in May of

2014. We lost a few of our leaders during the transition and I had to build from scratch however, in less than 6 months I was able to build a team larger than ever before in my career. As I write this, we have over 1,500 representatives in 16 States and Canada. Our organization is growing every day and we will reach millions of people over the next 3-5 years either through the life essential services we offer or the business opportunity. I attribute all of the abilities and success that I now have to the personal development I have undergone over the last 10 years and having great coaches and mentors who see things differently than I do and that have walked the path to success before me.

Having learned about a good work ethic at a young age has always served me as an entrepreneur. When you are accomplishing goals and chasing dreams you are usually not going to see instant results, so having Applied Faith and persisting when it seems that it is not working is a major point to study and understand. I am sure that you have heard the adage "Nothing is more powerful than a made up mind", and that is as true today as it was when it was first spoken. Once you have made the decision to pursue your ultimate goal or dream make certain that you reinforce that decision every single day with actions you take towards it.

Lay out your goals in bites - daily, weekly, monthly, 90 days, annual, 5 years, and 10 years. Make sure they align with your ultimate goal and purpose. Once you have your ultimate goal in mind and your plan of action, review them often and make sure you are on track to achieve them.

Another key to focus on is the Mastermind principle. Make sure that you surround yourself with people that support your goals and have goals and dreams of their own. If you fly with eagles then you will become an eagle but if you hang with chickens you will not leave the ground for long.

There are a lot of average thinkers out there and this is something I learned at a young age. When I told people as a teenager that I wanted to be a restaurateur they laughed, chuckled, and sneered, because they had not known anyone that owned a restaurant in their teens. As a matter of fact, most of the people I was surrounded by at that time worked in restaurants because that is where I spent most of my teenage years working and some of them were much older. At the time I could not understand why they did not believe me, when I told them I would be a restaurant owner. Most people measure achievement from their own perspective. If you spend time with small achievers they cannot fathom having more than they have ever had so it goes against their instincts to believe bigger than they have ever achieved. When you come in with big a vision and dreams that will conflict with their beliefs, they try and talk you out of it. Not because they don't want to see you succeed but because success is so foreign to their mindset. They feel like they are protecting you by talking "sense" into you!

A question I am often asked is how are you able to stay so motivated, and the answer is simple. The key to motivation in my opinion is motive, in our industry we call that your Why. In "Think and Grow Rich" it is called your burning desire. My why is to help retire my parents and allow them to live the life they have always dreamed of without worry or strife. Because my why is so personal to me it drives me every day to get up and make it happen by any means necessary. I suggest that you find out what your why is and make the commitment to do what it takes to make it a reality. Start with your why and make it so big that yesterday dies, and nothing can ever stop you.

Another major component that has contributed to my success is learning how to raise the B.A.R. in his life. B.A.R. stands for Belief, Action, and Results. Here are a few keys that you can learn and implement to raise the B.A.R. in your own life.

The first key is to design a picture of your life that you simply cannot live without. Ask yourself what the dominating picture is in your mind. One of the handfuls of coaches I have learned from says, "You don't get what you want in life. You get what you picture." Most people want incredible success, financial freedom, and the freedom to pursue their passion, but they never take the time to picture it.

Therefore, they never take the action steps to obtain what they want. Every single day, you must place in your mind a picture of success. Designing what your life looks like and putting it down on paper is vital to raising the bar in your life.

By taking three steps every day towards your goal, you can attain anything you desire.

First, you must design and build your life in your mind, write it down on paper, and you have to take massive action to physically build your desired life.

The second key to raising the bar is to determine what inner conflicts must be resolved in your life to accomplish your goals. This is the step that average people tend to stay away from, the action that will cause the results. One cannot say, "I want to be wealthy, rich, successful, etc.," and watch TV all day long. Something would have to be removed from your life to make room for something greater to move in. You will be making a decision to make a sacrifice for your long-term gain.

You must decide that there is no turning back and you must burn the ship of retreat. Napoleon Hill in "Think and Grown Rich" said, "There is no such thing as something for nothing." This is something you must decide immediately. The Latin of the word decision literally means, "to cut off." Making a decision is about "cutting off" choices – cutting you off from some other course of action. Now that may sound a little severe and limiting, but it is not. It is liberating.

The third key is to find a mentor. A mentor is the only exit from the past. You can either learn from your personal experience or learn from the experience of another. A wise man once said to learn from others mistakes because you wont live long enough to make them all yourself. A mentor is a champion who believes in you and, more importantly, you believe in them. Every person who has ever raised the bar in his or her life or won in any undertaking has had the great gift of a mentor.

Your mentor will give you a living and breathing picture of success. When you find a mentor, do not take them for granted! When I found my mentor, I did not yet have the success I was looking for. With the guidance of my incredible mentor, I became a National Manager and top earner in less than two years. I made it my focus to learn from his experience and allow his mentorship to lead me to phenomenal success.

Creating a plan and taking action is the final key to raising the bar in your life. Once you have put your plan of action on paper, you must continually execute the first three keys and continue to work your plan until it becomes your reality. Until you see the desired results, your actions must consistently continue. In creating this plan, you must have the right tools, strategies, and skills. These will come based on how well you execute your first three keys in raising the bar and increasing the standards in your life.

Finally, having a Definite Purpose is the most important tool one must have to accomplish dreams and goals. My skills and coaching strategies have been proven to help hundreds of individuals to obtain a six-figure income, and that's just the beginning. My definite purpose is to produce one thousand six-figure income earners through the industry of network marketing before the age of thirty-five, and be remembered in as many testimonials as possible.

BIO

Having worked in restaurants since age 11, Daniel Zykaj always knew he wanted to be his own boss, and after high school he went on to own a restaurant by age 19. Never having gone to college, Daniel started his first network marketing experience before the age of 20 after being introduced by one of his customers at the restaurant.

By the age of 29 he has reached the very top of the network marketing industry and is among the top 5 income earners in the fastest growing network marketing company in the industry today. Daniel credits his success, after years of failing forward in the industry, to the incredible mentorship and coaching of his mentors and other leaders he worked with in the past 10 years.

From these dynamic leaders he has learned several principles that govern how to create wealth. Today Daniel has taken these principles, along with several wealth-building philosophies and is now coaching and mentoring hundreds of thousands of individuals to lead the financial revolution.

Mentor. Coach. Leader. These words have been used to describe Daniel Zykaj, but, as a "Do It First" leader, Daniel has focused on one major philosophy; "Help enough people get what they want out of life, and in return you will have everything you want out of life."

Over the years, Daniel has helped and shown thousands of people all over the world to dream big and more importantly that those dreams will become a reality with hard work and determination, but above all teaching the principle that YOU BECOME WHAT YOU THINK ABOUT.

You can contact Daniel Zykaj at:

(586)549-7558

danielzykaj@gmail.com

www.DanielZykaj.com

THE FIRST VOICE
By: Shaniequa Washington

As I've moved forward and accepted the things I have been called to do, the challenge has always been understanding the voices that surrounded me. The meaning of sound, vibrations that travel through the air — or another medium — that can be heard when they reach a person or animal's ear. The distance the sounds traveled to reach me was surreal. The influence of sound is so critical in the nurturing process of finding oneself.

In December 2005, while learning to become a strong leader, I experienced something that led to many moments of thought, times of reflection, and soon turned into a decision. The difference that I experienced was the inner voice. Many call that voice instinct or a hunch, or intuition. Napoleon Hill calls it the sixth sense. I have learned as I look back that it really was a divine purpose of the Holy Spirit guiding me into all truth.

The truth was that I was more than my circumstance, I was more than my failures, and I was more than my disappointments. The Shaniequa L. Washington you know now — store manager, author, evangelist, business leader, conference host, leadership developer — is not who I was. I was broken, hurt, lost, disappointed, and ashamed, and all of those voices prevented me from meeting my destiny. Growing up as a child, I was repeatedly told to do the right thing, but was never shown any true example of the right thing to do. Exposed to the constant use of drugs and alcohol by those who were entrusted to care for me caused me to learn what the voices of rejection, poverty, failure, and isolation sounded like. I adapted and learned to live in a void, unable to identify with the voices of success, passion, greatness, and confidence. I accepted the idea of settling, reinforced by compromise and dysfunction, as this seemed to be the most common sound I knew.

But as I got older, there was something else that grew; it was the voice constantly telling me that I could win, I could change, and it is possible. The problem was the other voices that constantly warred with the voice of hope and promise, and caused me to retreat. I can recall countless times trying to press forward, only to be told, "You are going to be just like your mother, a nothing, a drug addict, and you will never have anything." I soon began to wonder if I should accept that call, the call of failure. Fortunately, it was always the voice on the inside that would speak to me and give me great ideas at the most opportune times and would connect me to the right people. I had to learn to speak to myself and listen to my inner voice, the one that created passion and the desire to break the cycle of regression.

One of the most memorable times of my life goes back to December 2005 while working in Charleston, South Carolina under great leadership. I was given the opportunity to stand in as an acting store manager for my general manager, who was on vacation, and the inner voice said, "This is your time; I will bring you before great men." I recall tuning in passionately to receive instructions. I heard the voice say, "You need you to get this place into better shape than before your manager left." I remember the outside voices of other individuals saying, "You are crazy. I am not doing that. I will not kill myself." At one point the voice of doubt showed up and began to talk to me: "Is it worth it? What will it prove? What is the gain?" It was in my moments of quiet time and praying to God that the inner voice said, "Leaders do what others will not do. Leaders do what others refuse to do. Leaders are trailblazers; they pave the path." The 'go for it' voice spoke so loudly that it was hard to ignore. Before I knew it, I had completely yielded to the task at hand, showing that I had what it took to run the store.

I remember in full detail the intense tour of the store, the meetings with various associates, and getting them amped up about what we were going to do. I positioned it as the thrill of showing that we were committed, that we were willing to reveal our true nature and determination even when no one was watching or challenging us. I allowed the Holy Spirit to guide me throughout the entire week. I realized that listening to the voice inside, instead of the outward voices, opened a portal of elevation. I was promoted one year to the day of my previous promotion and ended up running my own facility.

This created the voice of trust. I learned through this process that God speaks to me and has a plan for me, a plan for me to prosper. But after all of the interviewing and finally accepting the position, the voice of fear beginning to speak to me again. This promotion was a dream come true because it was not only totally unexpected, it was also historic. I had blazed a trail, becoming the first female store manager in the demographic area, behind a history of all male Caucasian managers for over 20 years. The promotion required me to move more than three hours away and leave all that was familiar, comfortable, and understood. Fear began to speak loudly. "Who will care for your children if something happens? What if you get there and it does not work? What if the people reject your leadership?" Then the inner voice stepped in. "Shaniequa, I will never leave you or forsake you. I have always been here with you. Look back at where you have been. Have I not ensured you were ok? You were always covered even when you did not know me."

I had to begin having conversations with the Lord, asking Him to strengthen me, help me, and connect me with people so that I would not feel alone. I yielded once again to the voice in me and moved to Beaufort, SC to run my first store for the No. 1 company listed by Forbes 500 — Walmart. The store I was chosen to run was initially a challenge. There were many underlying issues with poor foundations that had to be restructured. I arrived excited, ready to go, and ready to win. But to get there and experience obstacle after obstacle was wearing me out mentally and physically. The voice of mockery showed up and said, "Ha, so you thought you could bring your little self into this town and make a change. Good luck." The outer voices began to point out all of the failures, including the managers before me who could not succeed. They said, "It has always been this way. Nobody has ever been able to make the change."

My inner voice began to say, "Shaniequa, I need you to walk by faith and not by sight. I need you to believe in what I have established. What I have put together no man can tear apart." It helped me to understand what Napoleon Hill shared in his book, Think and Grow Rich, that faith is a state of mind and that it may be induced by self- suggestion. I began to tell myself, "Shaniequa, when you come into work, you must take dominion of the atmosphere and you must be the glimmer of hope that will encourage people to yield to the light of what is new. You must illuminate them." I again found myself yielding to the voice, reminding myself daily that faith is the only known antidote to failure. Napoleon Hill was very instrumental in sharing that faith is the key ingredient that, when mixed with prayer, gives one direct communication with Infinite Intelligence. I now knew how to listen to the voice of faith, and that I had to believe to receive.

Things soon began to transform. The team was onboard and tremendous changes took place. The store was recognized on many levels for its evident improvements. I soon saw that yielding to the inner voice opened a portal for elevation. The voice of faith began to speak and said, "Shaniequa, now that I can trust you with small things, I can now trust you with greater things and I will increase your capacity. However, always remember that to whom much is given, much is required." I soon said farewell to that store and the awesome team that had developed. My last day was filled with so many emotions as the team marched from the front of the store all the way to the back. I stood in awe with tears streaming down my face. My team walked to symbolize the march in Birmingham, like Dr. King did. They allowed me to see that I had brought them so much peace. That day, each associate shared a personal message while releasing a balloon in the air as a symbol of higher heights for me. It was such a humbling experience and I heard the voice ask, "Are you ready?" I responded, Yes, I am ready.

I moved to my next location and it was not the same as the other store. I did not have as many challenges, and the people were more accepting, making it much easier. One morning as I was conducting my routine tour, I came into an area of the store and a person began to speak. "What are you so happy about all the time? I think you are faking. Nobody could ever be that happy. I don't trust you." I recall beginning to hear the voice of questioning and self-doubt, and began to ask myself if I did something to cause this to happen. I wondered what I could have done to cause this person to feel that I was not genuine or real.

For the next couple of weeks I was very distracted and overlooked things. I even began to entertain certain negative voices. I heard the inner voice say to me, "You are peculiar and set apart. You will never fit in." As I heard this, I wanted to listen but I felt conflicted. I felt that I needed to be guarded, but did not want to ignore the voice that had always been right in my life. I yielded to the voice that made me feel on guard and before I knew it, associates complained and began saying that I was unapproachable, mean, and did not have their best interests at heart. I was angry with myself for listening to the voice of compromise. I had compromised who I really was because of a voice of misunderstanding, a voice of interruption, a voice of confusion. I now was in war with myself, trying to find my way back to a place that I had already established. This is when I truly understood the idea of yielding to perfect will or permissive will. I wanted to be in the perfect will of the Lord.

Throughout this year I was attending church and while there, I received the word that my spirit was not filled. One Sunday afternoon while driving through town and spending time with the children, I felt a strong pulling and the inner voice said to check out that church . I obeyed the voice as I had a much-needed desire to be refueled and recalibrated. The following Sunday as I was preparing for church, the inner voice told me to visit that church. I told my family that we would visit this church and my children responded positively because they did not feel free at the other church. I was baffled because until that morning they had not shared their feelings with me. As a family, we entered the sanctuary and I was immediately consumed by the feeling that there was an awesome presence that was inviting and loving and so peaceful that I just wanted to sit and rest. The inner voice said, "This is your new home. You will grow here. Remember when you told me you were ready?" I paused and said, Yes, yes, this feels good. I am ready. I attended the new church on a consistent basis and soon joined Love House Ministries as my new place of worship. It fulfilled and edified what was speaking on the inside of me.

At work things were getting better and I found myself receiving specific instructions from my inner voice about re-establishing relationships and rebuilding teams. I remember coming to work one day and calling all of the associates together. I told them that I had not been a good leader, that I had allowed circumstances to influence my judgement, and that I cared for my team too much not to formally apologize to them. Did I win them all? Of course not, but most of them found humility in my apology. I attended Love House for a few years and was growing tremendously. As I grew in church, I grew at work. I remember my inner voice telling me that greater days would soon be here. I did not really know what that meant for me so I just accepted it, but really did not think about it. One day I had to respond to my inner voice, which reminded me that I had said I was ready, that I was being pruned and prepared to accept yet another promotion because of that yielding to the voice.

In 2011, I was being called into the office of the fivefold ministry as a minister. This moment takes me to a point in Think and Grow Rich where Napoleon Hill reminds us that "life's battles don't always go to the stronger or faster man, but sooner or later the one who wins is the one who thinks he can". Responding to the voice of faith strengthened my belief that all things are possible in Christ. As I accepted the call of minister I faced more voices, but this time it was totally different. It was magnified and constant. Voices that were the sound of judgment, isolation, conviction, condemnation, religion, self-righteousness, and bondage. The voices were more prominent and persistent than other voices I had conquered. These voices were everywhere. I heard them at church and at work. I had to become more intimate and submerge deeper, seeking a way that I never experienced before. The true voice that resided in me had risen and I had to begin to speak what was inside me and to command what stood before me to flee. I had to be sharpened so I could discern THE voice amongst all of the other voices. This turned into times of trial and error, and there were times I withdrew because it seemed to be never-ending. I had always journaled and now I heard the Holy Spirit. The voice in me (the Holy Spirit) directed me to be disciplined in my journaling, to rise early to seek Him, to pray and fast, to deny myself of my own desires so that I would be able to hear Him clearly above all else. For three years I lived a totally consecrated life and I was constantly seeking and listening for specific instructions. As I yielded to His voice, with the guidance of my spiritual leaders, I heard the inner voice say it was time. In 2012 my dreams began to come to me stronger than ever. I dreamed of standing in front of people with a microphone in my hand. I woke up excited and wanted to share. The inner voice said not to share and to put this in my journal and time stamp it until I was told to release it.

I have a fear and reverence for the Lord and was not willing to not obey, so I placed it in my journal and said no more. In that same year the inner voice spoke to me and said, "I dare you to be different. I have not called you to be common, you will not worship like anyone else, lead your store like anyone else, and operate in ministry like anyone else. I have called you to be the difference that inspires, creates peace, and prepares the unsaved for greater." I was so excited and wanted to share and again, the voice of the Lord forbid me and told me to lead by example and that others would follow. I followed the instructions of the Lord and worked hard to ensure that I was conscious of my decisions. I owned my failures and I addressed things quickly in harmony so that those watching would desire to know the why behind my life.

It was just before New Year's leading into 2014 when I yielded to the voice as the Lord said, "Are you ready?" I said yes and a portal of elevation was opened as I birthed my first woman's conference, 'Dare To Be Different'. This was so difficult. I recall the voices that were not THE voice saying, "Nobody knows who you are. Who's going to help you? Your Pastors won't allow you to do this, and you can't afford to do this." The inner voice said to me, "Shaniequa, greater is He that is in you than he who is in the world. If I be for you no man could ever be against you."

I remember it so clearly. I went to talk to my Pastor who was excited for me and gave me the green light. I was so excited to go and talk to my co-Pastor, my pastor's wife, my spiritual mother to share the great news, and the inner voice said, "You are not allowed to share anything with her. From this moment forward, unless it is the team I coordinate, you don't share any detail with anyone." This was hard, it felt sneaky, and I felt like I had no guidance initially in my first big assignment, only to later understand that this taught me to totally depend on God's voice as no other voice lords over His voice. My first conference was sold out! We had to turn people away at the door. I was in awe and totally grateful to the yield.

In my yielding, once again there was a portal of elevation that created the branding of Dare To Be Different Empowerment. I wrote my first book, Leading From The Front. I am now entering into my third conference while hosting a four-city tour of empowerment workshops. What I found interesting is, I was always worried about balancing this and a demanding job in the capacity in which I operate, and the inner voice said to me, "Shaniequa, my yoke is easy and my burden is light, if it is my will provision shall be your portion." In yielding to this message that spoke so clearly to every portion of my being, I said, "Lord, I desire to be in your perfect will. I want it all." In 2015 the visions and dreams became much more vivid and I was astonished that God would share with me something at work, in Sunday school, in my journal, and literally what He gave me, my leaders would release from the pulpit verbatim and my boss would recite verbatim. The

Lord reminded me that He was only confirming what He spoke to me, that I would never deny myself of any good thing. The Lord said to me, "Shaniequa, I trust you!"

Towards the end of 2015, the inner voice said to me, "Now, it is now that you are to speak. I need you to open your mouth and command the atmosphere to respond to your voice." I began to declare that I would make the right connections and the Lord would bring me before great men. I declared that my husband and I would be a powerhouse couple. I declared that I would mentor and guide in leadership. I declared that I would be a number one bestselling author.

In yielding to the voice again, I received elevation by being connected to Tom Cunningham as part of this awesome experience. I am now in the process of developing my leadership development company, Zuriel Leadership, and I have been called into the office of an Evangelist and accepted the call. It is true as Napoleon Hill states in Think and Grow Rich; there are no limitations to the mind except those we acknowledge.

If I had acknowledged all of the voices that wanted to destroy me, you would not be reading this. There is an inner voice and it is constantly speaking to you, guiding you. That gut thing is whatever you call it. The matter is real, but what is even more real is your response. Know that there are voices that are always competing for rank, but know the first voice, the voice of God, which should always be number one in all that you do.

"But seek ye first the kingdom of God and all of his righteousness and all of these things shall be added unto you." Matthew 6:33.

Remember nobody can answer the call for you.

BIO

Shaniequa L. Washington is an author, speaker, mentor, and the CEO/Founder of Dare To Be Different Empowerment. She is also a Walmart store manager. Shaniequa has risen to management levels by providing illuminating leadership and showing people how to shake off mediocrity and live up to their greatness. It is a message Shaniequa has learned from her own life and one she is helping others apply to their lives.

Dare To Be Different Empowerment specializes in the delivery of personal and professional development enrichment programs that focus on adversity, communication, creativity, goal-setting, productivity, reinvention, time management, motivation, and leadership. Shaniequa creates and develops products and services that include but are not limited to seminars, workshops, curricula, and training for professional leaders, women in particular.

Shaniequa is the author of Leading From The Front. Her books teach readers the foundations of being a leader according to the Biblical principles founded and established for more than 2,000 years; it teaches readers to live an extraordinary life even in the face of adversity.

Her personal story talks about being a child living in an environment that the world would describe as a lost cause, with both parents on drugs and alcohol. Shaniequa chose to rise above all challenges, and her story is unique, as she has climbed the ladder of success beginning more than 19 years ago as a part-time cashier. She entered into the leadership world as a manager a mere two years later, and has been steadily climbing ever since. Shaniequa was determined to make it and she did without credentials such as multiple degrees and certifications.

This has been the core of her passion and leads her to inspire, encourage, and uplift women, to teach them to learn from their experiences and tap into their inner gifts and greatness.

Learn more about Shaniequa at www.shaniequawashington.com

AN UNSTOPPABLE JOURNEY
By: Shamla Maharaj

Imagine being born in a developing country like Trinidad and Tobago back in 1985 where no sensitization, or even a near thought of being disabled, existed and only the privileged from urban areas were able to access basic services. Picture not only that but being a child with severe Cerebral Palsy; having involuntary body movements, the ability to use one hand while shaking, and trying not to stiffen, kick or hurt someone. Picture being permanently confined to a wheelchair with restricted balance. Picture all of this, as well as growing up in a rural area where the only legitimate income was from farming, and substance abuse of all types was rife.

Firstly let me first be clinical and describe Cerebral Palsy (CP). CP is a neurological condition that affects movement and co-ordination. Effectively, it is brain damage, usually irreversible, caused by brain injury before, during or immediately after a child's birth. In my case it occurred during birth as a result of negligence. My brain was deprived oxygen as a result of being squeezed in which I did not cry but made a sound similar to a rat. This resulted in brain damage.

My CP is classed as chronic and I have only some control over a very shaky right hand and forearm. I have no control over my left hand and arm and it will occasionally flail out, all on its own, to strike whatever or whoever is on my left. I have no mobility or control over either of my legs. With no sensitization, I was stigmatized; being called crippled or retarded. Family members also knew nothing about education for a person with a disability and so confinement to a room was the epitome of what a person with disability like myself was entitled too.

As a child I never thought of myself as different I knew I could not walk but my family did all they could to include me, even my cousins. On the

186

rare occasions I could not play I felt sad and left out I felt but sadness never lingered in me I only allowed it at that very moment.

My father worked as a cane labourer and my mother, a domestic homeowner, sometimes woke at night and sewed in order to meet the basic needs of the home. I would often suffer the effects of alcohol abuse. I was definitely not spared from the 'rum-shop attitude', a 'rum shop' being the local bars where the workers go to get drunk on cheap rum after working. My dad who was deprived a full education himself envisioned me to be just like any other child whose rights and needs was to get an education. With my dad saying, "my child has to go to school" he sought information by asking others, and in the deep end of south Trinidad a place named Moruga was where he found the information he was looking for. This man who toiled as a labourer and was physically abused as a child, walked miles to learn that there was a place I could go named the Princess Elizabeth Special School. I was taken to the home and left there without my family for the sake of school.

Looking on as my parents walked away I lay in a crib at 4 1/2 years old, my back not strong enough to sit up. I remembered asking the nurse while crying "when are they coming back?". Left alone I knew that my worst nightmare as a child had come to pass. No longer wrapped in the security blanket of my family, consisting of my parents and 2 brothers, I had to cope from that tender age with learning how to deal with different people being my guardians, 3 different nurses a day, 12 a week on average, in charge of your daily functions.

Shy, timid and retreating into myself resulted in me being left thirsty in fear that asking for water would cause a burden and often emptying my bowels about only once per week. Not knowing my rights as a child and having to cope with the differing people was challenging.

The environmental change was a shock because with no form of transportation my family rarely went out. Leaving the deep rural areas of one end of Trinidad and going into the suburbs of the capital city. My parents took public transport to bring me to school, often being refused or kicked out of vehicles because of my disability. Cultural change, along with behavioural principles was new. I quickly adapted and was forced to be accepting of varying personalities.

This was not the only transition that was required to take place. Cultural shifts and behavioural change was necessary. My religious beliefs as a Hindu meant adapting to Christianity. Schooling proved to be the reason for sacrifice. I coped well and was always eager and willing to do what was instructed and required of me despite my involuntarily body movements and control restrictions to one side of my body. This is because I was always eager to be included and learn. Most times the pace of teaching was slower in order to accommodate my fellow classmates. This had to be dealt with because no other school wanted, or even entertained, the thought of accepting me.

Throughout my school years I was often excluded. Yes, I was excluded from activities in a "Special School". Excluded from field trips, because of the complexity of my disability, excluded from my religious beliefs and excluded from society, because of the institutionalized environment. Once in a while we would visit one shopping mall, which was the extent of the excitement in my life.

Persistence, determination and willingness was seen in me from an early age because always strategized a way to get involved and having family support and cooperation made the difference. I have learned coping skills, advocacy and decision-making skills, and cognitive skills. I learned lifelong lessons at my primary school, including basic manners, which are instilled in me today, and the fears I had turned into lessons. My common entrance teacher noticed my ability and insisted that I be included in activities and speech making. She made me the team leader and this awakened my outward ability. I graduated as Valedictorian and best overall student in 2000.

My dad had stopped drinking and with some encouragement from others moved out of the family business of being a cane labourer and became a crane operator in a contracted firm. I moved on to a Secondary school in my village. The fear of moving from a secluded society into "normal" society was at the back of my mind and lingered even though I always aspired to attend a "normal school" and return home every day just like my brothers.

The challenge started on day one when the Principal of the local village school opposed my enrollment. My Mom challenged them on the basis of "Inclusive Education for all" which was coined by the then Minister of Education. Excuses including having no desk available and no classroom space were made. It was quickly counteracted by my Dad saying he would build my desk and that I only needed a little space.

Two ramps were built by my father and brothers to get to the downstairs classrooms and suggestions were then put forward by parents and I, who was just as alien to the situation as all the other parties involved. The school timidly accepted our idea of having classrooms brought upstairs. I questioned my potential and ability when I entered and saw what I had to cope with. I went head on, although I often missed labs and extracurricular activities. I felt sad but I often reassured myself that I would get through. The teachers eventually understood me and I did not allow anything to keep me from coping with the pace of other students and my willingness to be treated like anyone else in the room. They took it upon themselves to have me involved and never questioned my ability to compete.

The actual schooling was not the only challenge I had to face. I took it upon myself to condition my body to use the washroom once per day, which required training. This benefited my mother and myself. My mother's tolerance and patience was often pushed to the limit during this phase of me wanting to adapt my body. After a few months my body adapted and still benefits me up to this day.

At form 3, I was awarded best overall student in my class and in the year 2005 I graduated with all passes. I was then accepted into lower 6, which was a surprise because I never thought I would have reached that far but I carried on. I lobbied along with 3 other students to have a course taught at senior levels. I was the only student who did the course combination and therefore was not able to attend 1 course. I still passed all Units for all my advanced level courses.

Going from one level to another I never had precise goals. I decided on one goal when I was a child: to be a success, work and be independent. With the little I money I received and saved as a child, along with a disability grant, I often bought things I needed. My parents worked hard and sacrificed to fill any void to ensure I received my human rights. I made a little go a long way, which was a moral, instilled from my mother. I signed up at the University of the West Indies (UWI) because others did. I was already prepared to take a few courses in a school, which might of advance me further but I did not even know if the school was accessible. I was settled to do this because we saw no other way due to accommodation and past successes of a disable person. I knew however, I wanted something out of life and in order to get it I had to achieve what was presented to be currently.

I would revert back to when I was in primary school, I remember one weekend watching a television show at the home I stayed in and I saw a man clad in a professional attire working in his office commanding his own environment and I told myself I want to work in an office too. I had no clue how to get there but I knew the first stage was to pass my common entrance exam and attend a high school. This would also achieve another goal of mine, which was to be able to go home every day just like my siblings. The steps I took to achieving my goals was never a huge one rather I thought about the goal at hand and succeeding at that and then moving on.

The day had come when UWI put out an advertisement calling on all students who have applied to come in and view the acceptance list, mom and myself second guessed on going thinking we would not have gotten through. We still went and to our surprise my name appeared on the first listing. I felt profoundly proud of myself because I never thought such a thing would ever happen. My mother and siblings toiled with me to get me started. Nothing was in place to cater to a person with a disability. There was no handicapped accessibility at all. If I had been left alone I would never have made it through the first day.

Because handicapped accessibility was not available I had to go up three flights of stairs to class. Not even the Dean or Academic Advising and Disability Unit (ADLU) knew its precise functions when it came to facilitating Persons with Disabilities (PWD). Again we had to suggest and put forward possibilities of what could be done. From year 2 classrooms were being brought to accessible buildings and in Year 3 after showing that I would not let a simple inaccessible pavement or journey stop me, I saw inclines and ramps, all my classes were put into strategic locations. My faculty began to be very helpful and compromised a lot; even ADLU learnt from my challenges and used it to tremendously help others that followed. My lecturers would come outside and meet me and even took it upon themselves to ensure accessible classrooms were made available to me. I never took no for an answer I have lived the word of alternative, if I could not reach a table I used a chair to write on, if one pathway was not accessible I used the longer pathway or even the road. I went there to learn not to find excuses.

Do not expect the world to facilitate you if you are not willing to adapt yourself. Let's face it, life is unfair and full of stumbling blocks, some prevalent while others you create. However, live in such a way that you do not set yourself up with fictional thoughts. Rather, realistically know what challenges you are going to be faced in life, given your present circumstances and set your life up in such a way that when those challenges hit you, you can combat it with just one choice, which is you want to move on and move up in life. There is a whole world around you and you must believe in your confidence of who you are and what you want out of life. I have never made a complaint one day about what was presented to me, rather I personally sought my own solutions. You can do anything you want once you have a strong willed mind. Up to this day I am trying and that is all we can do is try our best move up and move on. I am restricted physically yes but my mind isn't so I use it to the best of my ability and believe me wonders will happen.

It was difficult having to deal with the commute to and from University in order to accommodate my siblings' even though I rented one of the University Dorms with my mother we had to share parental guidance. Being deprived of many nights of study because of the problems of alcohol abuse was my greatest challenge. The burden would be relentlessly placed upon me when my mother felt frustrated, and such frustration was taken out on me. I often had to justify my rights to my parents to do core courses because it sometimes became overwhelming to them because they too had their lives to live, which was infringed upon.

I have learnt however, through my challenges domestically to block away negatives immediately after it has happened because dwelling on it would only allow it to get to you. I deal with it there and then and moved on, some things you cannot change therefore, you adapt in such a way so it would not stay in you and affect you.

After all of that though, it worked out. I graduated within three years with a BSc in Agribusiness Management. I went on to complete my Master's degree MSc. Marketing and Agribusiness (Business and Marketing Analysis specialization). Having to commute to and from university required my family taking time off from their own busy lives, which required a lot of compromise from them. I now move onto my PhD in Agricultural Economics (Marketing and Agribusiness Specialization). My philosophy is to do your best in order to progress and keep moving on.

Graduating in 2010 gave me public exposure and I was featured on the front page of two major newspapers. This not only empowered me but also made me aware of and educated about disability statistics in my country. It has motivated parents to have hope for their child with a disability and it changed my life and my family as we now all volunteer time for motivational speaking, advocacy and being spokespersons for groups.

In 2011, I was assigned as a Social and Disability Ambassador and in 2012 I was asked to represent persons with disabilities at UNESCO's Second Management of Social Transformations Programme (MOST) Conference which was being held in Trinidad. I was carded to speak on behalf of PWDs, which I was elated about. After my speech, which was witnessed by The Assistant Director General of UNESCO, she said I should represent my country at their 8th UNESCO World Youth Forum in 2013. I was elated but really did not believe it would happen. One month before the actual forum I received an email from UNESCO inviting me to their 8th World Youth Forum in Paris. I was wholeheartedly happy and at the same time scared because I had never travelled out of the country. For one month I got everything together I needed. I told myself that everyone probably had to go through the same thing not knowing what was to come. On the first day of the forum I was ushered into the VIP room thinking it was only protocol then I was escorted out only to look up and see thousands of youth staring up at me. I really did not know I had been chosen to be the opening speaker. I sat among five fellow opening speakers including the Director General. As my turn to speak approached, I felt as though my head was spinning with thoughts and that I had to represent my country well. I spoke from my heart and I got a standing ovation. I was approached by many people from across the world and I was humbled at the thought that they would get to know Trinidad and Tobago. That very night I was still overwhelmed that Trinidad and Tobago was on that stage. I wanted to make the most of it and during the debate I made sure I contributed which made it into the introduction of the final report to be presented at UNESCO's General Conference.

I am currently employed in my second job. Getting my first job was a challenge. It took me 3 months to start work after acceptance. Like before, a tour was facilitated and suggestions for my accommodations were made. My qualification was often questioned. Thankfully my supervisor went to university with me and therefore duties and responsibility were assigned according to my qualifications and competency, which I proved highly. Now I am onto my second job. I still search for something that will help me be more independent and help me achieve what I have always wanted to do, which is to be independent. I have started my own consultancy business and intend to work hard because having a disability is not cheap and I also want to have nice things in life and to pay for them with my own hard earned money. One day I want to be able to write about what I have accomplished and not my disability and I continue to work towards that.

I must say it is difficult wanting to achieve so much and having to depend on my family physically to have to lift and carry me from one point to the next. It is a challenge and puts a strain on them. I have many goals however; living in a country with no handicapped accessibility is indeed restricting. I have to give up some things because my family simply has their own lives to live.

Recreation has also been a challenge and like everything else I am restricted because of handicapped accessibility. I one day want to be able to do and go anywhere I want, when I want and how I want. I want to be able to afford it, which I cannot right now because of mere access. I have all the ideas to achieve this level of independence and I work day in day out, set goals beyond my capacity in order to achieve financially, which is the realistic way of gaining independence.

I say to others who wait for things to happen or wait on others that you are blessed with the faculties to help you function properly. You have both hands and both feet, you are able to lift yourself, and you know how much you can do. I say therefore, why feel sorry for yourself or even depressed, do things to uplift you and others, take yourself up and go places. If could of you know how much more I would of done. I am never satisfied I always want to do more and see more.

194

Although I have come a long way, I still feel that the journey has not yet started and there is still a great deal of unchartered ground to cover. I will continue to advocate for change, for acceptance and INCLUSION. My ultimate aim of life, to be independent and pave the way for others behind me is still ongoing and will be a lifelong process that I will never give up.

It is scary knowing my mommy is getting older and that I quickly have to personally grow to get a sustainable job to help with my independence. I now live to make my late father proud, live up to his name and carry on his legacy, which requires constant hard work. I love my country so much and I hope that one-day that I am given the opportunity to help charter positivity in Trinidad and Tobago and beyond.

BIO

Shamla Maharaj has had Cerebral Palsy from birth, but has never allowed this challenge to deter her. She is insistent about proving to her country of Trinidad and Tobago that a person with a disability can live a full life once the opportunity is created, as she has done with the unswerving support of her family. Being a motivator and advocate, Shamla has left positive impressions on institutions and minds with whom she has interacted and her plan is to continue doing so. She is also sensitive to the topic of poverty. Although her field is primarily the promotion of food sustainability through business and marketing, she would like to see all of her interests including equity for persons with disabilities and poverty alleviation fit together like a jigsaw puzzle however for now she will continue to address each cause individually.

Shamla has a Master of Science Degree (MSc.) in Marketing and Agribusiness (Business and Marketing Analysis Specialization). She recently started her own consultancy business with the aim of helping the sector while helping herself become more independent. She is currently a PhD candidate for the Agricultural Economics (Marketing and Agribusiness Specialization) program.

Shamla has experience in the Agribusiness sector as she sat on the Advisory Council Board for the Ministry of Gender, Youth and Child Development.

She also served as Social Ambassador and Social Motivator for the Ministry of Social Development in which she spoke to various groups in society. She also represented her country at the UNESCO'S 8th World Youth Forum where she was the opening speaker.

Shamla can be reached at 868-389-9079 or by email at maharaj.shamla@gmail.com

DON'T SETTLE FOR SUCCESS
By: Gina Best

Twelve years ago, when I launched my first business, I read a book that set the pace for my success: Think and Grow Rich by Napoleon Hill. Today, more than a decade later, Hill's Principles of Success are still woven tightly into the fabric of my business, its vision, and its success.

Success is a funny word that really has no definition. It is subjective, yet we look at it as definitive. Based on money in the bank and number of fancy cars in the driveway. But is that really "success"?

It can be, however I believe it is so much more. Most people consider themselves successful by the dollars in their bank account. But they are wrong. I know, because I was wrong for a long time. I measured success by the wall of awards in my office. The more awards, the more success. After all, an award-winning mortgage broker is a successful mortgage broker, right? Our company went from $0 - $130,000,000 in 12 years. I was personally awarded the "Best Mortgage Broker" in Vancouver numerous times. I also won community awards. Clearly, I was someone important; I had the proof. The awards said so. The money said so.

Still, with all of the financial success of my company and the ever-growing wall of awards, at the end of the day, in the quiet, as the shadows danced across my desk, I would hear a whisper "Is this it?".

I ignored it. Brushed it off. I fought back against it. I mean, How could this be? I had it "all". Great business, money in the bank, healthy and happy kids, lots of friends, and a huge social circle. That is the definition of "success" right?

Wrong.

The voice in my head screamed: "You are greedy! You are selfish!" And I listened. I actually believed it. So I continued what I was doing: more work, then rushing home to be mom. And in every other teensy pocket of time between Work and Mom, I filled the gap with doing things for others. I was the go-to person for my network—and my network was big. I made sure everyone else felt grounded, supported, happy, and taken care of. Everyone that is, except me.

I was not my own priority. Not even close. Likely not even in the top 20.

Big mistake.

Question for you: Where do you fall on your own priority list?

Really think about this. Do you put yourself first? Have you ever asked yourself what the cost is to you when you do not put yourself on the priority list? (Trust me: it's B-I-G.) There is a hefty cost: physically, emotionally, mentally, and maybe even financially every time you put yourself on the back burner. I know this from experience. It was a hard earned lesson.

Let me explain.

I got married in 1997. My husband and I wanted to start a family. So we practiced – a lot. Which, naturally, was a whole lotta fun! Fun as it was, it was not working. When the natural way did not pan out, we went to a fertility clinic. Our luck changed and we got pregnant with twins. When I told my husband, it was like Christmas Day. He was elated! But the excitement eluded me. Deep down I knew something was very wrong.

At nine weeks, I had sharp pain and lots of blood. An ultrasound confirmed that I was still pregnant, but now only with one.

On a Friday, another 9 weeks later, at 4 1/2 months pregnant, I felt off. I had a sinking feeling that something very bad was happening. That weekend I was very still. I was afraid to make any sudden movements. Terrified that if I did, this baby would leave me. On Sunday, he did. It was early in the morning. The inexplicably horrible pain woke me up. And in our hallway bathroom I delivered my son. I pushed him into this world and he would never take a breath.

In the hospital later, I had surgery, sympathy cards, and a loss I could not deal with. I could not even speak about it. I would not, to no one. When I lost that baby, I lost a piece of me – the voice of my emotions. I became cold, stoic, detached. I did not take care of me.

For a long while, I avoided everyone and everything. I slept all day and stayed up all night. I did crafts like an addiction – just to keep me sane. In December, I made clove oranges. Hundreds of clove oranges. For the record, no one has a need for hundreds of clove oranges. It was a distraction, anything to avoid thinking about and feeling my loss. In January, I went back to work. And I never talked about what happened. EVER!

I went on to start my first company; it was my baby—one I could grow. I gave it everything I had. I nurtured that seedling into a multi-million dollar empire. I threw myself into work. I filled my days with being busy. I made sure that every minute had a purpose. I did not want to look inward. I did not want space to think about me, my heart, my walls, my losses. I was my last priority. So I kept going.

And I was amazing (or so I thought). Like I said, I had the awards to prove it. I was successful. I was happy. I convinced myself that I was great. And in this fake euphoria, with a big ol' elephant under the rug, my husband and I decided to grow our family. We adopted two amazing boys. "Success" was everywhere: financially sound company and two healthy thriving boys! My days were full; my heart was void. But I could not see it yet.

I kept growing the business. I worked tirelessly. I strived to be the perfect mom. (Ain't no such thing!) "Busy" was my religion. I was doing it all. And yet, the whisper continued to pester: "Is this it"?

I continued to ignore it.

In 2013, I decided to start another company – more time at the office meant less time dealing with my shit. They say ignorance is bliss for a reason. I jumped in, took a leap of faith, got the license, hired a great partner, and pressed GO. Then I freaked out. How was I going to do this?! What was I doing?!

Around the same time, I had a visit from a friend who normally had this crazy energy about him—and not in a good way. It was madness. This day, however, there was an obvious and dramatic change. He seemed totally at peace with how he was for the first time ever. It was so calming.

So I asked him about it. He told me about a program that changed his life. A few weeks later, I applied and was accepted to Dov Baron's Authentic Speaker Academy for Leadership. I had no idea what I was getting myself into. It was so terrifying that I literally had to put my head between my knees when I signed on the dotted line. I was frightened. I knew in my heart this was something I had to do.

So I did it. And found myself, a few months later on a Thursday morning, pacing in a hotel lobby—freaking out, again. I was trying to muster up the courage to walk confidently into a room full of strangers, tell my story, and let my life shift. I knew the moment was going to be life changing. I knew I needed to let go. I knew I needed to be honest, let down my walls, and be vulnerable. (Ugh, the V word. My nemesis!) I breathed deeply, swallowed fear, and walked through the door.

That weekend changed everything.

E-V-E-R-Y-T-H-I-N-G.

It was 6:01 pm on Day 3 when Dov stood before us and asked one poignant question: "What is your biggest shame?" Shame? Pssh... I don't have shame, I thought. I was FINE, totally FINE! I did not do shame. I spent years avoiding that feeling in the pit of my stomach. A tiny little voice whispered: Gina: The babies. My head screamed NO! But my heart took the reigns, and I took the microphone and spoke for 16 minutes about something I had no idea I had attached such shame too. In that moment the wall I spent years building, crumbled to the ground. Fast. Furious. Crash. Boom.

I stood in front of a crowd and shared the secret I had kept to myself for 15 long years; the secret of shame and of not being enough. I was completely exposed.

The shocker was I had no idea that I had been keeping this secret. It was buried so deep I had no idea it was there. Yet once I let it out, the relief I felt was unbelievable. The clouds parted. I could see and feel clearly.

The weeks that followed were a blur. Letting my secret out meant that it ALL came out. I was an opened faucet. The grief that I had held inside so tightly for years began to seriously kick my ass. At first, I fought it. My mentor looked me in the eye: "Gina, you have to go there." With conviction, I said: "I do not want to go there". But, once you learn something about yourself, once you set your secrets free, there is no going back to that locked place.

So I went there.

I revisited the past—reluctantly. I kicked and screamed my way through it. It was not pretty and it was not easy. It came to a head when I was on a trip without my family and the grief swallowed me whole. I just simply could not fight it anymore. It hit me like a freight train. It took me to my knees – literally. I was at Club Med in Cancun, Mexico and I spent hours on my knees in the shower, sobbing for the babies I never got to hold.

It was my lowest moment. And it was the moment that helped me rise.

It was the beginning of a huge change for me.

Keeping busy was my way of hiding from the real stuff. Busy was my way of coping with heartbreak and grief. But there was no real coping. And there definitely had never been healing as a result. Busy meant I could face all sorts of other challenges on a daily basis so that the real challenge—my true feelings—could sit in a corner and gather dust. I was too busy to acknowledge them. Busy was my ultimate excuse. When I was busy, I was in control. If I unlocked the vault where my grief was, I would lose control. I would be vulnerable. During the course, the big joke became "Gina doesn't even know how to spell the word Vulnerable". They were right. I avoided vulnerability. Easy, right?

Easy? Yes. Good for me? Absolutely not. I hid behind a huge personality, bright hair, and big social circles. Yet I did not share myself with others. I used my tongue as my sword to keep others at bay. I used a maxed out calendar as an excuse to avoid feelings and just kept going.

I knew I was missing something; I just did not know what it was.

The journey exposed the truth: I was missing me.

It felt like there was a clock strapped to my back and I was always going. There was never enough time for me. I ruled my life by my schedule and if there was a gap in time, I filled it with a new problem, activity, or person. I was not present for myself or anyone around me—including my kids. A weakness that hurts deeply to admit. After wanting children more than anything, I was choosing to keep them at arm's length. Even those little loves of my life could not penetrate my wall. I was in a perpetual mode of self-preservation and protection. From everyone.

Everything has changed. My life is so different now that the first 43 years of my life are like a distant memory.

My company is thriving. Financially speaking, 2015 was my best year ever. I worked 80% less and earned 37% more. When I am sitting with clients, we talk about mortgages and planning like always, but we also talk about life authentically. Clients share their lives with me. The more open I became, the more open they became. My business relationships thrived because they were real relationships. Not long ago, a young couple shared with me their fear around the health of their child, who may be diagnosed with Down's Syndrome. That is big stuff. Heavy stuff. And they shared it with me. A sign, I'd say, that opening up gives us the capacity to have richer relationships.

Now that I am present with others, more people are coming to me for business. I built my business on referrals on purpose. I love relationships and honest conversations. Now, however, my referrals are different. They are not just business based, like "Gina is a great mortgage broker. Go see her." They have substance. They are based on my character, too. It is so much more rewarding to have connections on a deep and authentic level with new clients. A level where they feel heard and feel safe to talk about what is going on in their lives – so I can do more than just help them find the money they need, I can connect them to their dreams. At the end of the day I am far wealthier for making true connections than for making deals.

We have had the best two years ever and are still growing. I discovered my "Why". I know now why I do what I do.

Like I said: Busy was my religion. it was my everything. And it was a poor decision to live that way for so long. I do not ever want anyone to walk in those shoes – they look nice but they are uncomfortable and will lead to a lifetime of bunions folks! I want you to have the freedom to connect with yourself and with others. To truly go for it in life, even if going for it means wading through a big pile of emotional shit first. I want you to know that it is okay to feel good, to feel bad, to feel sad, to feel stuck. It is okay to experience the highs and lows. Because you are alive, and life can be sticky, and it is also the very best gift we will ever have. You are enough and you are allowed to dream big.

My own journey led me to step back from my mortgage brokerage. Turns out, it is not my love; coaching is. So I coach and speak, because I love it.

This journey has been a long one, filled with hard earned lessons. All of which I learned from and grew from. My skillset has grown. My confidence has skyrocketed. And today I get to do what I truly love: Empower business owners to build the success they choose. In fact, my business card says "Coach, Speaker, No Shit Taker," which makes my heart sing ever-single time I pass one out. That's me – the woman who does not hide any more.

I speak to groups. I share my story. I get that you can be successful and lost at the same time. And that there is this beautiful thing called free will – we have it and we deserve to embrace it. You, too, deserve to do what lights you up inside. You have the power to choose your next move and to be the author of your life.

BIO

Gina Best is a serial entrepreneur and a maverick coach with a penchant for pushing people's buttons and compelling business owners to deal with their personal shit so they can attack their businesses with passion and authenticity. Gina owns one of BC's largest mortgage broker alliance, runs her own business building workshops, coaches entrepreneurs, speaks to and inspires audiences across the continent, and still finds – rather makes – time to be a mostly patient mom to two wild boys, a witty and wonderful friend, a shoe hoarder, and a bold and gracious mentor to young business women in her community. Gina is the first to admit that she has it all and she earned it – through hard work, tears (like full out sobs), anger, self-doubt, grit, and hustle.

To contact Gina e-mail her at gina@gina.best or call her at 604-340-3600. Also check out her website at http://gina.best

THE POWER OF PRAYERS
By: Nancy Lee

JOMNAN

That was the name my grandma gave to me when I was born on December 2, 1972, in Battambang, a province in northwestern Cambodia. When I was only 2 years old, on April 17, 1975, we were attacked by Pol Pot's troops, the Khmer Rouge, my grandma told me.

In case you haven't heard of him, Pol Pot was a leader of Cambodia from 1975 to 1979. As soon as Pol Pot took control of Cambodia, he imposed a reign of death and terror upon his own people. It is estimated that during Pol Pot's brutal communist Khmer Rouge regime, over two million people died, including my grandfather, my father, two uncles and their families. Many people died from disease, starvation, overwork, or execution. Their mass graves are known as the "The Killing Fields." Many of the survivors suffered from starvation, trauma and poverty.

To this day, I still don't know the real cause of the killings. A part of me doesn't want to relive the memory; a part of me is still in denial, and yet another part believes it was all just a bad dream.

After all, aren't we all living in a dream? Some people say life itself is a dream, and we only wake up to reality when we die.

I was too little to remember much about what happened to my family. My 75-year-old grandfather was too old to work for Pol Pot, so the Khmer Rouge let him starve to death. They tied my father to a pole that supported our house. My mother told me that she sneaked over from where she was working as a slave laborer and talked to him. Pol Pot's soldiers were indeed savage. We never saw him again.

Sometimes in the next few chaotic years, my mother remarried. My stepfather was abusive -- he beat my three sisters, my mother and me. I don't remember when he first began to mistreat us, and I lost count of how many times we got beaten. Domestic violence was common in Cambodian households even in normal times; it was usually thought that the victims deserved to be disciplined.

THE DEAD ASLEEP

In 1979, we were somehow able to escape to Thailand with other families. We walked at night and hid during the day. One night, I remember, as we walked in single file with only a little moonlight to see by, I tripped over bodies in our path and thought, "How can these people be so sound asleep that they don't wake up when we walk on them?" I didn't realized that these were corpses, people killed by the Khmer Rouge.

Another night we were walking through a swamp, trying to be really quiet, when my right leg began itching. I stopped to look at it. A dead leaf seemed to be stuck to the front of my leg. I tried to wipe it off. But minutes later my leg felt itchy in the same place, so I tried again. Even when I pulled hard, I couldn't remove the thing -- and then I realized it wasn't a leaf but a blood-sucking leech. I screamed. A man from somewhere in the back of the line rushed over, grabbed me, covered my mouth with his hand and told me to shut up, but I was so terrified that I couldn't stop screaming and kicking my legs. Finally the man pulled out a pocketknife, scraped the leech off me and sliced it into pieces to prove to me it was dead. After that, I refused to walk, and my uncle carried me the rest of the journey.

KHAO I DANG CAMP

We made it to the Thai border safely. Like other refugee families, we put up a tent and lived there for a while.

207

One day my mother heard that Thai and U.S. aid agencies were allowing senior citizens and small children to board a bus and be moved to a much better camp, Khao I Dang, farther away from the enemy, where food and shelter would be provided. My mother knew she would't be allowed on the bus; she would have to stay behind with my stepfather and my two young sisters. But she told my older sister and me to get on the bus with my grandmother, saying it was our best chance for survival. This meant we might never see each other again.

At Khao I Dang, a "holding center" for Cambodian refugees, people helped us build a shelter of palm leaves and bamboo. Food was provided weekly: a few cans of sardines, packaged noodles and some uncooked rice. The number of people in each family determined how much food we got. We were also allowed a bucket of water per person per day. The bigger the bucket, the more water we got. Most people had five-gallon buckets- - a heavy burden to carry on our shoulders during the four-kilometer walk from the water source to our shelter.

I remember crying myself to sleep every night. Not only had I lost my biological father, I was separated from my mother and younger sisters. I prayed to be reunited with them, and my prayers were answered. Very early one morning I was awakened, and there they were -- my mother and the rest of my family.

THE NIGHTMARE CONTINUES

During the next few years, we left Khao I Dang, moved to several other camps and then returned to Khao I Dang, Not by choice, but by the Thai soldiers. Finally, in 1986, we made it to Dallas, Texas, thanks to my family members in America who sponsored us.

The nightmare of living in Cambodia under Pol Pot, and later of living in refugee camps, was over for us. But the nightmare of being abused by my stepfather continued.

208

I remember coming home from a school at a camp we moved to in 1982 and seeing my mother's face covered with black and blue bruises. Her eyes were swollen so badly that they remained shut for days. I felt angry and helpless because I hadn't been there to protect her. Yet when I was home and tried to interfere, my stepfather would beat me up too. I would scream at the top of my lungs to get the neighbors' attention -- It was the only way he would stop beating us.

A year later, back at Khao I Dang, my mother went to visit my grandma. She asked me to watch one of my younger sisters so my stepfather wouldn't abduct her while she went to work. I watched, all right, but I couldn't stop him from grabbing her. I ran after him for miles, pleading with him to leave my sister and the rest of us alone. I ran and ran until I could no longer follow him and lost him in the distance.

My mother tried to leave the relationship many times, but my stepfather kept convincing her to return to him, and he kept beating us. What I could never understand was why his two adult sisters would just stand there and watch him do it, with smiles on their faces. Never once did these women try to stop him.

In America, at least, there were child safety laws; I was happy and relieved to know he couldn't hurt us physically anymore. However, he did not end his verbal abuse.

After Dallas, we lived in a housing project in Los Angeles, California. I started to pray to God to let me get married so I could finally escape my stepfather. Back then; marriage was the only way a Cambodian girl could leave her parent's household. I just wanted to get away from all the abuse. If I couldn't, I would kill myself. By the age of 16, I had already attempted suicide four times. During one of the times, I was treated by paramedics and ended up in a hospital bed.

My prayers were answered again. My longtime boyfriend agreed to end my misery by marrying me. And so I got married, right after high school.

But I can't say that I lived happily ever after, because a whole new set of problems arose. I had a mother-in-law from hell; and, unexpectedly, my husband turned out to be an abuser too -- mentally, emotionally and verbally.

Six years and two wonderful daughters later, I decided I had endured enough. I had been insulted and taken advantage of for far too long. I decided that I should raise my girls on my own. Right after I graduated from Brooks College in Long Beach, California, with a degree in fashion design, I left my husband.

I was scared. I didn't have any money. But I had to make a bold move. By then, my mother had finally divorced my stepfather. She was living in Providence, Rhode Island, with my siblings. I wanted to be closer to my family, where my kids could grow up with their cousins and I could eat my mother's cooking again. So I went East and moved in with my younger sister Angela.

Life was hard, raising my two girls, Lala and Somer. We walked through the snow to my older daughter's school while they younger daughter was in a stroller. We cut up black trash bags and used them as raincoats. We wore donated jackets and made the best of what we had.

I struggle to find jobs, but I couldn't give up. That's what my ex-husband wanted to see. He wanted to make sure that I suffered so badly that I would go running back to him, begging him to take me back. He wanted it so badly that he didn't give us any financial support for his children.

One or two jobs weren't enough for me, because I wanted to move out of my sister's house. So I took four jobs — one full time, and three part time, as a freelance Interpreter, a waitress and an interpreter at the

Providence Center, an out-patient psychiatric facility. It was very hard, I didn't see my kids much, but my older daughter was going to private school and my little one to the best day care. I didn't mind working four jobs because I wanted my kids to get the best education possible so they wouldn't have to struggle like I had.

By 2005, I'd had enough of the snow and I was physically worn out. I made a deal with my ex-husband in Long Beach: I would drop the child-support case I had filed against him three years prior, if he let us live with him until I was ready to move out on my own. He agreed. So I packed whatever we could fit into six suitcases and my kids and I moved back to California.

There, too, I struggled to find a full-time job, but I did land a few contract jobs. It seemed that I'd just complete one when I'd find another.

In 2009, God finally answered my prayers again. This time I'd asked Him for a great man who would love my girls and me and who would be able to provide for us so I wouldn't have to work my butt off like I had for so many years.

THE PRINCE CHARMING

I met my Prince Charming when I went to an advanced electronics firm, Pioneer Circuits, to give a presentation on the need for schools in Cambodia. In the fairy tale, Cinderella left her glass slipper at the ball. In real life, I accidentally left my jacket where I had given the presentation. The president of the company, James Y. Lee, made certain that I got my jacket back.

Over a year later Jim and his assistant visited Cambodia. He thought of me during his return trip to his home and decided to email me. He asking me to join him for dinner at the Da Vinci Restaurant near the Long Beach airport.

I greeted him with a hug, and we talked for three happy hours. Jim admitted later that I'd stolen his heart with that hug. It was a fabulous first date and I remember it like it was yesterday. We got married six months later. God knew I needed a super hero in my life, and He could not have sent me a better person.

James Lee swept me off my feet and took my girls as his. We have been living happily in Southern California ever since. I can finally have my happy ending and fulfill my dreams of helping others in need.

Together we help many Cambodian organizations, include building schools in Banteay Meanchey, Stung Hav Sihanoukville and Tatia Koh Kong, through the Summit Foundation of Cambodia or Moulitek Edung in Khmer, which my husband and I set up. This foundation provides youth leadership and give scholarships to high school graduates so they can continue their education.

SENIOR SUICIDES

In many years of volunteering at a seniors' center in Long Beach, I heard story after story about Cambodian seniors committing suicide at an early age -- during their late 50s or 60s. It broke my heart. I couldn't understand why people who had survived the cruel Pol Pot regime of hard labor and a tiny cup of watery rice gruel per day would end their lives in this country, where all kinds of services were available to them. I tried to make sense of it but couldn't find the answer.

At the same time, there was all kinds of chaos among both young and old Cambodians living in Cambodia. I wanted to help them too. But how could I, when they were on the far side of the ocean? That was the big question.

THE NANCY LEE TALK SHOW

I remember an unreal moment I'd experienced in 2014 when, for the first time, I visited the set of Ellen Degeneres' TV show in person. I was a huge fan of hers, and I thought how wonderful it would be to have my own show and my own set. Then I laughed at myself and brushed the thought aside.

At the same time, though, my husband was thinking about having a television channel and Web site where he could provide educational and empowering materials to a mass audience. Suddenly a light bulb in my head switched on: It was clear that I needed to have my own show.

But how? Who would watch my show? Except for a few months of acting classes when I was in high school, I didn't know anything about show business.

Then I read Napoleon Hill's book "Think and Grow Rich." It told me that if I had enough passion and determination to make it happen, it would happen.

I visited my friend Paula, who owns Angkor travel business in Long Beach and saw a postcard advertising KhmerTV. I looked at it but didn't pay much attention. A few days later, I had lunch with another friend, who was watching KhmerTV. Again I didn't catch on. Then I met a third friend who told me her parents were hooked on KhmerTV -- they watched it all day long.

That's when I realized I was being sent a message: I needed to have my show on KhmerTV. A local channel that needs antenna or online streaming.

I asked this friend if she knew the owner of the channel. She said yes and told me that he and his wife were very nice people. I opened my purse to get my wallet and pay for lunch -- and there was the KhmerTV postcard! I couldn't remember putting it there, but there it was.

Right away, I phoned the number on the card to set up a meeting with the owner. I asked for only 30 minutes of his time -- if he didn't like what I had to offer, I wouldn't waste any more of it. Somehow I knew he wouldn't refuse me.

We met. I was nervous but determined. I explained that I wanted to create a show that would bring positive messages to non-English-speaking people about body, mind and soul and about connecting the old with the new generation.

He said he had no money to pay me, but he would support my idea and be willing to pay his staff to record my show once a month for a six-month trial. I told him I would find my own crew, a location to film in and guests to be on my show. We made the deal in 15 minutes.

I knew I wasn't going to make money. In fact, I would have to use my allowance to pay for the set, snacks for the audience, dinner for my crew and other expenses. But I didn't mind. I would be chasing my passion; I would bring positive messages to my people in my language, and I wanted to end seniors' suicides.

I told my best friends about my ideas, and they were willing to make time to get on board with me. We recorded the first Nancy Lee Show in November 2014, just 10 months after I'd sat in the audience at Ellen Degeneres' show. Our first guest was the legendary Khmer actress Virak Dara, one of only a few Cambodian celebrities who had survived the war.

I'm happy to say we have finished one full season of the show and have reached a worldwide audience.

I wanted to thank my husband, James, who believed in me and always encouraged me to be the best version of me and serve others full heartedly. I also want to thank my children and friends, who sacrificed their time for my cause. KhmerTV and I are still paying out of our pockets to record the show, but many people have benefited from it. We feel we are on the right track. Since 2015, we have not heard of another senior suicide — again, one of my prayers answered! I will never underestimate the power of prayer. It often works to create a miracle.

BIO

Nancy Lee is a philanthropist, an International Facilitator for youth leadership and the President of Dream Beyond Foundation, a 501(c)(3) nonprofit organization based in Santa Ana, CA. The foundation was founded in 2014 to serve the under-served Cambodian seniors in Long Beach, which has the highest concentration of Cambodians outside of Cambodia. The foundation also provides scholarship to Southeast Asian youth to further their education.

Nancy Lee has taught hundreds of youth how to reach their full potential and to adopt good habits. She is an independent licensed Facilitator for Path4Teens through Laurie Beth Jones and The 7 Habits of Highly Effective Teens with Franklin Covey. The Principal at Rongko high school, in Banteay Meanchey, Cambodia, commented that "Nancy Lee is the best Facilitator I have ever met in my career."

Nancy and her husband, James Lee, have built three school buildings in three provinces in Cambodia. They are also the founders of the Summit Foundation in Cambodia, which provides shelters for children from remote rural areas of Cambodia to attend a private school in Phnom Penh. It also provides scholarships to high school graduates and teaches the youth leadership program.

With KhmerTV in Long Beach, CA, Nancy Lee launched The Nancy Lee Show in late 2014, with the aim of promoting awareness, preserving the Khmer culture, and connecting the old and the new generations. She has said: "I've never failed to offer a helping hand. I might be broke helping others, but I'm very rich in my heart. That's what success is all about."

You can contact Nancy at:

dbfinfo@yahoo.com

thenancyleeshow@gmail.com

TRUST THE PROCESS
By: Amy Thomson

I had a pleasant childhood, according to my mother. In spite of living in a physically sound environment, I seem to remember a lot of crying and hiding in closets. I felt I was and was hard on myself when I made mistakes.

Those thoughts and feelings plagued me for years. I took them with me all through my adolescence and into adulthood. It did not matter how many friends I had, how many people complimented me or told me they loved me. In my head, I was unlovable.

Of course, not knowing the power of thought, I made a lot of poor choices. On the bright side, I now clearly understand the intense power of thought and what it can do to one's life. In fact, I teach it to others, including my kids because everyone deserves the benefits of sound positive thinking and peace of mind.

A Personal Example of the Effects of Poor Thinking on One's Body

I was sick a lot as a child. I spent many days on my grandma's couch or home with my babysitter. I remember sometimes being so fearful of things happening at school that I would actually make myself sick. I did not realize it was my mind's way of avoiding something I did not want to deal with. So sickness actually was preferable to me than whatever was happening at school.

What I have learned is that the more a person thinks a thought, the stronger it gets, until it becomes a belief. Additionally, people act according to their beliefs, so unless we intentionally train ourselves to think better thoughts and learn to plant them into our subconscious minds, our beliefs will continue to run us.

My thoughts persisted until they became beliefs…my 'story'. "I'm sick, weak, nobody likes me and I can't do anything right."

Obviously, with thoughts like that, my future was pretty predictable.

I was sexually explorative at a young age (wanting to feel loved); physically, sexually, financially, and emotionally abused (I believed I was a victim); had anxiety and depression (no surprise); and attempted to take my own life (it was not worth anything anyways); and was a serious alcoholic by the age of 15 (why not?). When I tried to quit drinking, I'd resort to mild drug use to take the edge off (nothing heavy). By the time I was 19 and my classmates were hitting the bars, drinking was no longer of interest to me. I was already on the road of self-discovery, personal development and a better life.

In the meantime, I had two mild strokes, almost 60 cavities (Yet somehow, I still have a beautiful smile :)); and became allergic to virtually everything I ate and everything environmental. I had leaky gut syndrome, hormonal imbalances, ADHD, Fibromyalgia, Chronic Fatigue and Insomnia (at different times), and two life-threatening pregnancies. And I am still here! Not only that, I'm thriving! I have no pain and have not been on medication in years.

The Power of Desire

Desire in me is strong. SO strong.

Even with all of my personal development training, which I started taking in my teens, after my attempted suicide, my 'weak, sick and worthless' STORY would continue to surface. Deep down, I knew it was not true, but my illnesses continued to get more frequent and severe, as I grew older. I did my best to ignore them, which was a terrible thing to do. Neglect and dwelling on the negative will both make things worse. By the time I was 32, I had become so chronically ill that I thought I was going to die before I was 35.

Well, I am happy to report, I am 35 now and feeling better than ever! I fully believe I will get healthier, stronger and more attractive as I age.

A major turning point for me was when my daughter's principal made a subtle, but clear threat to get children's aid involved and have my kids taken away from me because they were frequently late for school. They were well fed, housed, clothed and loved. And yes, they were often late for school. My life was led by pain and fear, and many days were difficult to move or function properly, even though I was trying my best to get better.

I lost it. I cried. A lot. I threw my hands up in the air and my face into my pillow and said, 'I surrender! Whatever I have to do, I'll do it!"

With absolute conviction, "I am not going to allow any of this to control me anymore. There's no way in hell I am not going to be here to raise my kids! I will do whatever it takes to be around for them, with them and be the best parent I can be. Yes—I am going to beat this! In fact, I am going to beat this and every other obstacle I come across. I will show my kids they can overcome anything. In fact, I will become a beacon of hope for anyone, going through anything. I will live my life on my terms and achieve my dreams, so I can show others that it is possible!"

The feeling of certainty and determination was intense. I went from having a desire to having a burning desire and a definite major purpose (DMP). Not long after my resolve, a friend called me and said, "Amy!! I have the answer! I met a woman I believe can help you! She is a very busy homeopath, but I can get you in. Come with me tomorrow and bring a list of your entire health history."

So that is what I did. I wrote a few pages of things I had been through health-wise and went to meet her. I was not even sure how to pay her. I had already spent so much money for things to supposedly 'make me healthy', and they obviously were not working.

I put my total trust in this stranger and spilled it all. I shared my traumas, feelings, thoughts, and fears...everything. I did not hold back. I was a sobbing mess all over her desk. And I pushed through my embarrassment because I knew what I wanted. My purpose was stronger than any feeling I could endure.

Sure enough she did help me. She helped me with my diet, which I thought was impossible because I reacted to almost everything I ate. Because of my pain, I barely slept and although I had quite a bit of background health knowledge, she helped me connect the remaining dots between mind/emotion/body, food, environment, vibration and energy.

She helped me to understand that I had attacked myself for years in my thoughts. My body was just following the direction I had given it. Now, I had some work to do to undo and reprogram myself.

A Brief Update

I did the work and almost ever think about illness anymore. If it creeps into my mind, I dismiss the idea and think about how good I feel and how lucky I am to be in my physically active, healthy and attractive body. I have had only one cold in a year and no other ailments. If I get an ache or a pain, I know what to do to make myself feel good right away. And I just came from the dentist with a glowing report card. All A's...and no C's (Cavities)! This is awesome!

Another thing that makes a major difference is that I AM living a life of my own design, and a life of purpose. I am excited about getting up every day and doing what I do. I know life IS a gift. I do not want to waste it. Sometimes I wake up at two in the morning because I am so excited to accomplish something I am working on. I have recreated my own beliefs and reprogrammed my mind for success in all areas, so that is what is showing up. I really can see myself getting stronger, more attractive, healthier and wealthier as my life goes on.

Back To My Story

My poor thinking previously attracted poor health, negative relationships, abuse, financial difficulties, depression, anxiety, and a myriad of self-destructive habits. I was often taken advantage of and had no trust in myself, others or anything in this world. I second-guessed everything. That was until I learned the power of decision.

Decisions Must Be Clear and Definite

Before learning and applying the philosophies in Think and Grow Rich, most of my decisions had come through painstaking crises. For example, my decision to grow rich came from seeing the impact of my parent's separation on them and the family, when I was 11 years old. I decided to become financially independent and not have to rely on a man to take care of me. When I was 26, that idea went out the window when I gave birth to my disabled daughter, and found myself suddenly losing my business. I found myself dependent, without an income and suffering from serious sleep deprivation and postpartum depression. Recognizing there could be a better way, I discovered money could work for me and I began learning about passive income.

Also, I was 21 when my dad died. I noticed he did not get to live his dreams. He wanted a sailboat so he could travel and meet people. He was so close to retiring.

His death left me feeling like he was ripped off. I saw him working so hard to take care of the family. When he died, I had a lot of questions. It did not make sense. What was the point of his life? One question led me to another. And most importantly, my father's death led me to find my definite major purpose--To discover my purpose, live my potential, and love my life.

Rediscovering Self

I knew when I was a child I was here for something big. I just knew it. I was going to do something important for the world, and on a big scale. The feeling continues to grow. I no longer fight it. I just go with it. That is likely the biggest reason I quit jobs I had. I did not feel I was providing a meaningful enough service to enough people, or there was little left to learn and challenge me there so I would move on. I wanted to use my abilities to their best potential. People would look at me, call me names and tell me I was a failure, and I just knew I was destined for something better.

I realized it was unlikely I would find a job that would allow me to constantly create, learn new things and solve social problems on a massive scale, unless I was aligned with similar people like myself, which used to be a rare thing to come by. So, I decided to create opportunities myself, where I could use my talents, create opportunities for people to live into, and provide value for millions of people worldwide.

Napoleon Hill taught me that I can have anything I want, as long as I am clear on what it is, demand it of life and have full faith I will receive it. If I need clarity, I can always tap into infinite intelligence to find the answer.

Ask, Expect, Allow and Receive. Always, Without Fail.

I believe I have always had the ability to tap into this power. I learned the skill from my parents, but only knew it's potential regarding my schoolwork. I had not used it for anything else. In fact, when it came to anything else, I was the queen of indecision and did not trust my own judgment. I was continually told I was naive and gullible, so I did not trust my instincts. How silly of me!

It was not until I started reading books like Think and Grow Rich, The Law of Attraction, Frequency and The Secret that I understood the power of my mind and my thoughts. Since then, my entire world shifted. I trained myself to ask, allow and trust. It was difficult at first, but anything worth doing is challenging in the beginning. Through practice, I have become clear on how to do this and use it many times per day. I quickly became clear on why I am here in this world and what I want to do.

Lessons and Unfolding

My path has been slower than I would have liked, but there were lessons I needed to learn. The unfolding was necessary, no matter how much I wanted everything all at once. Answers came in little dribbles at first, and now momentum has picked up and wonderful things are happening. I am excited everyday to have mini miracles happening all around me.

All I did was adopt the success principles into what I was already doing. I kept asking questions to bring clarity into every aspect of my life and did the work to reprogram my subconscious. I continue to do this daily. Because of this, I easily take actions every day that used to be difficult for me, but no longer are. They are in line with my purpose and intentions. I am attracting the right people and circumstances to make things happen.

I am aligning myself with other creative problem solvers because I fully believe that ALL of the world's problems are solvable in multiple ways. I think one of the keys to solving them is to have people connecting with their true selves and living their higher purpose. I know part of my purpose is to help make this happen.

Being Tested

When I am tapped into my higher potential, I am a master problem solver. I can create anything and connect with anyone. I believe everyone has gifts they are meant to use and share, and in doing so, they become happier, more likely to collaborate, and peace on earth is becomes a real possibility.

I have created many products & services to serve this purpose and although I have done so, I recently faced a major adversity that caused me to step back and re-evaluate everything I was doing, only to find it made my purpose and belief stronger.

Last year, I was in Las Vegas, finishing writing the 30 Days to Happiness Program. I was really excited about it and had worked on it for a long time. The day I had finished writing the last of the content and exercises, something I never imagined would ever happen did.

My boyfriend and I were at the airport during a crossover on our flight home and he got a phone call we will never forget. Our sister-in-law was dead, his brother in jail, his truck seized and his house locked up for a criminal investigation. She had been murdered.

There was nothing we could do. We felt stuck. We could not go anywhere and we could not get a faster flight home, like they do in the movies. It was the craziest thing ever and we could not understand it. She was only 29, everybody loved her, she was a great mom and she was my friend.

It was an awful situation that I would not wish on anyone and I still do not understand it, but it happened. And we had to deal with it. My boyfriend's niece and nephew moved in with us and we went from having 4 kids to 6 kids in a small house. Then his sister moved back to the city to take care of the children and they have now recently got their own place, but the dust still has not settled and the court investigation is still in process.

This entire experience made me question every single thing I am doing. It tested my strength and definiteness of purpose.

I thought, "Okay great! I'm clear on my purpose. I know where I'm going.

"I'm creating all of these wonderful things to help people be happy and live their biggest dreams... I'm going to solve depression; I'm going to solve self-defeat; I'm going to solve anger and hatred. I'm going to cure illnesses; bring peace, love and joy to everybody..." and then I find out this happened. And I think, "Oh my God? What is the point in me doing any of this when I can't even help the people in my life that are close to me? Are these things always going to happen anyways, no matter how much I do? Is this world too big for me to take on? Who am I to even think I can make a difference anyway?"

I started to second-guess myself, this entire world and wondered why I had to continually be tested?

It has been said that when you are about to be successful, you will be hit with some kind of extreme challenge or adversity. And this was definitely an extreme adversity.

Is It My Choice? Or Am I Chosen?
After some time, I got clear that this is why I am doing this. This is why I wake up every day and do whatever I can to help the world become a better place. Because 'Hurt people hurt people' and I do not want anyone to hurt. Or hurt others. It is not necessary.

Take A Moment To Visualize
Imagine no wars; No reasons for people to be angry. Imagine people being so preoccupied with their true purpose that they have no time to spend on

hatred. They recognize their importance and value others. People are working together, using their unique gifts and loving their lives.

Everyone would be happier, less judgmental; not be causing trouble, and everyone would be contributing something wonderful to the world. We all have gifts we are meant to use, things we enjoy; even if we do not know how, what or why yet. And even if some of us have become so detached from ourselves that we forgot what we even enjoy.

John Lennon was so on the mark when he wrote Imagine, which also happens to be one of my all-time favorite songs.

"You may say I'm a dreamer
But I'm not the only one
I hope some day you'll join us
And the world will be as one"
-John Lennon

A Beautiful New Love

When my boyfriend and I had those two amazing little children come to live with us, I took to them as if they were my own. I loved them, and still do, unconditionally. I was willing to do whatever it took to make them feel loved, safe, appreciated, and at peace. I truly believe their mother's spirit came through me, because I cannot explain the sincere, nurturing and loving connection I had for them. I have never loved anyone else's kids as naturally as my own, until then. I helped take care of the family and their needs while everything was happening, despite it being a tense, scary and catastrophic time. But, I think that was my place.

Adding Fuel to the Fire

Since then, my intentions have become even stronger. Now I have even more reason to help people. I began to practice directing my thinking even more and working to directly influence my outer world through my inner world.

I started to align with many people who have similar visions and missions as mine. A lot of these people were already established or they had passion and belief so strong that it was obvious that they were going to succeed.

I have attracted partnerships, opportunities, people, money, resources, entertainment, and guidance--pretty much everything I focused on, asked for and allowed. I attracted the opportunity to coauthor a book with a bunch of amazing people who are also thinking and growing rich. And I even attracted winning the entire Think and Grow Rich Course Curriculum from the Think and Grow Rich Institute. That was fun!

Here is how that happened:

I was at Marcos Mendosa's I.M.P.O.S.S.I.B.L.E. Edutainment Seminar, which was fantastic, and Satish Verma from the Think and Grow Rich Institute was speaking on stage. He was opening up the Think and Grow Rich Institute in Toronto and giving away an entire course curriculum to one participant from the seminar. I would estimate there were a few hundred people there. I knew I was ready. I wanted it. It was time for me to move forward and share my gifts with the world. I was broke at the time and determined to win.

There was something different in my thinking that day. My habitual self would have created some excuse for me not to believe; to think someone else was more deserving than I—or something like that. But, that day I said

227

to myself, "If everyone has the potential to create their own reality, regardless of what others are doing, then the reality I create is not taking away from anyone. They can all win, totally independent of me. Today, I'm creating MY reality, and in my reality, I'm winning this!" And that's exactly what happened.

Before I could win though, there was a memory-testing question. Marcos asked the audience, 'In what year did Napoleon Hill interview Andrew Carnegie?'

I was so excited; I jumped out of my seat and shouted, '1908!' before he had even finished asking the question. Then I was called onto the stage to give the definition of a mastermind and the difference between desire and burning desire. I answered them successfully and won the course curriculum. Yay!

A White Hot Desire

I already had a burning desire. I was determined to achieve my objectives or live out my purpose in life. The main thing I was missing was a mastermind.

At that seminar, it became apparent how crucial a mastermind was. I immediately put that into my thinking but did not know how to find the right people and have a successful group.

So, I bought a copy of Napoleon Hill's Think and Grow Rich book when leaving the seminar and read it like a textbook, carefully studying and implementing what I learned into my life, including setting up a mastermind.

I wrote my clear and definite purpose, what I wanted to receive monetarily and what I would provide in exchange. I created a definite date and plan. I read it daily and took immediate action. Things began falling into place and I was on a roll.

With each course I took, I allowed the TAGR philosophy to sink in a little more. I asked a lot of questions. I allowed myself to be vulnerable and let go of any fear I had sharing or asking questions on any topic, because I was there to learn. It was not a coincidence that I won that program. And I was not going to let that opportunity go to waste.

I immediately began applying everything I learned into my life. I formed my first mastermind group and wow! What a difference that small group of people has made in my personal and professional life! If I only knew it's potential before!

A Mastermind Alliance is totally key. That is when 2 or more people are working together in perfect harmony toward a common definite purpose.

Not long after forming my mastermind, my business team came together, I started making more sales, getting more coaching clients, creating more products and services, graduating school (again), investing in real estate, and making a lot of new like-minded friends. I was also nominated for the Top 40 Under 40 Business Award, which is a big deal in my community.

Note

-Within minutes of me typing that last sentence, I got a phone call announcing that I have been selected as a recipient of the award! Another example of how thoughts become things! :)

I attribute the successes I am having to following Napoleon Hill's 17 Principles of Success, as well as learning from other experts in various fields. Some of the people who have influenced me and my work are: Wayne Dyer,

Louise Hay, Esther & Jerry Hicks, Tony Robbins, Bob Proctor, Greg Kuhn, Brad Yates, Robert & Kim Kiyosaki, Jack Canfield, Richard Branson, Walt Disney, Wallace Wattles, Maxwell Maltz, Oprah, Ghandi, my friends, family and mentors, and the list goes on and on. There are SO many people I learn from. I have made a point of learning from every person and experience I have ever encountered, whether good or bad. There are always things to learn.

I have learned that the faster I learn and apply the lessons, the less time I have to endure uncomfortable situations.

"The lesson continues until it is learned."
-Unknown

One of the most difficult things for me was to do, was to take my big dreams and plans, and put them together in a nice little package that was relatable to others. People saw me as lofty, unrealistic, and scattered. Some still do. And I don't care. I know what I want and where I am going.

It used to be frustrating. It was not until I started associating with more people who had larger visions and who had completed significant projects, that I was able to put the pieces together.

Ordinary people in my life told me that what I wanted to achieve 'could not be done.' And I did not believe them. Instead, I looked for people who believed otherwise. And I found them. And we are making things happen.

It's funny. I can so easily help people gain clarity and direction in their lives and put the plans together, but when it came to my life, I found it more difficult. The good thing is that I was smart enough to recognize that I needed help and I took the steps necessary steps to find it.

Now, I continue to work with coaches and mentors, and I refuse to give into stories. I stay focused on my plan and accommodate changes as necessary.

I take time regularly to connect with myself and tap into infinite intelligence. I intentionally feel the vibrations of things in and around me so I can continue to move into better and better circumstances, know the right answers, make definite decisions and feel confident in my life.

I bring these same skills and energy into my work and teach others to do the same. It's really powerful, enjoyable and relieving.

I am a Happiness Coach, Artist and Project Developer. I am a creator (as we all are), and I teach people how to tap into their creative potential to discover their purpose and dreams. My clients learn how to use the Law of Attraction successfully, reconnect with their higher potential and build habits that actually make happiness long lasting in their lives. This is all second nature to me.

I also create projects that serve the world and I seek out leaders to take them on. This way, people can develop themselves while living their passions and contributing to the world.

I bring positive energy, social contribution and the intention of elevating the world into all of my creative projects: Affirming Arts™ (Promoting Happiness, Healing, Authenticity, Community and Love into all types of media, such as Art, Apps, Books, Music, Programs, Videos, Workshops, Events, etc); FUNaTHON™ Multi-giving Initiative; and Empower 50,000 People Project. I am building a wonderful collective of creative minds who are working together to bring peace, love and joy to the world through their individual creative gifts.

Our collective is growing everyday and we are always looking for new talent and people who want to make a positive difference in the world. So connect with us if you'd like to be a part of it.

I am lit up everyday by possibilities. I really do love my life and everything in it. And I want that for everybody.

BIO

Amy Thomson is an award-winning creative director, happiness coach, artist, project developer, author and speaker. She owns Create.Build.Inspire.™ a company named after her personal mantra in life.

Contributing to people and the planet is entwined in everything Amy does. She has over 20 years experience with charitable and non-profit organizations in all capacities, as well as a strong background in personal development, project management, leadership and volunteer coordinating. She follows her creative flow and enjoys all arts, as well as nature and real estate.

Amy is the creator of Affirming Arts™, FUNaTHON™ Multi-Giving Initiative, Affirming Arts™ Creative Collaborative and the Empower 50,000 People Project.

Gifted at helping people discover their greatness, Amy inspires collaboration, allowing miracles to happen. She is committed to her two children and to bringing her social economic ventures to people around the globe, while keeping the roots of operations in Niagara where she, herself stemmed from originally.

Amy Thomson—Create.Build.Inspire.™ and Affirming Arts™

Connect with Amy at: www.AmyThomson.ca Amy@AmyThomson.ca or call at 289-696-2727

NAPOLEON HILL BIO

Napoleon Hill
(1883-1970)

"Whatever your mind can conceive and believe it can achieve."
- Napoleon Hill

American born Napoleon Hill is considered to have influenced more people into success than any other person in history. He has been perhaps the most influential man in the area of personal success technique development, primarily through his classic book Think and Grow Rich which has helped million of the people and has been important in the life of many successful people such as W. Clement Stone and Og Mandino.

Napoleon Hill was born into poverty in 1883 in a one-room cabin on the Pound River in Wise County, Virginia. At the age of 10 his mother died, and two years later his father remarried. He became a very rebellious boy, but grew up to be an incredible man. He began his writing career at age 13 as a "mountain reporter" for small town newspapers and went on to become America's most beloved motivational author. Fighting against all class of great disadvantages and pressures, he dedicated more than 25 years of his life to define the reasons by which so many people fail to achieve true financial success and happiness in their life.

During this time he achieved great success as an attorney and journalist. His early career as a reporter helped finance his way through law school. He was given an assignment to write a series of success stories of famous men, and his big break came when he was asked to interview steel-magnate Andrew Carnegie. Mr. Carnegie commissioned Hill to interview over 500 millionaires to find a success formula that could be used by the average person. These included Thomas Edison, Alexander Graham Bell, Henry Ford, Elmer Gates, Charles M. Schwab, Theodore Roosevelt, William Wrigley Jr, John Wanamaker, William Jennings Bryan, George Eastman, Woodrow Wilson, William H. Taft, John D. Rockefeller, F. W. Woolworth, Jennings Randolph, among others.

He became an advisor to Andrew Carnegie, and with Carnegie's help he formulated a philosophy of success, drawing on the thoughts and experience of a multitude of rags-to-riches tycoons. It took Hill over 20 years to produce his book, a classic in the Personal Development field called Think and Grow Rich. This book has sold over 7 million copies and has helped thousands achieve success. The secret to success is very simple but you'll have to read the book to find out what it is!

Napoleon Hill passed away in November 1970 after a long and successful career writing, teaching, and lecturing about the principles of success. His work stands as a monument to individual achievement and is the cornerstone of modern motivation. His book, Think and Grow Rich, is the all-time best seller in the field.

The Seventeen Principles

1. Definiteness of Purpose
2. Mastermind Alliance
3. Applied Faith
4. Going the Extra Mile
5. Pleasing Personality
6. Personal Initiative
7. Positive Mental Attitude
8. Enthusiasm
9. Self-Discipline
10. Accurate Thinking
11. Controlled Attention
12. Teamwork
13. Learning from Adversity & Defeat
14. Creative Vision
15. Maintenance of Sound Health
16. Budgeting Time and Money
17. Cosmic Habitforce